THE
ENERGY
ALIGNMENT
METHOD

WELBECK
BALANCE

ABOUT THE AUTHORS

Yvette and Lisa have been sharing the Energy Alignment Method® (EAM) globally over the last few years. EAM is an internationally recognized complementary therapy that has already impacted the lives of over 50,000 people worldwide.

Yvette Taylor is the creator of EAM. She has spent over 20 years using and teaching Eastern principles, spiritual practices and self-development in the UK and internationally.

She is a multi-award-winning transformational spiritual and business coach, international best-selling author, inspirational speaker, therapist, mentor and change-maker. She was voted as one of the Top 10 Holistic Therapists In The UK – *Holistic Therapist Magazine*, is a winner of the Janey Lee Grace Platinum Award, as well as multiple awards for 'UK's Best Coaching And Mentoring Business', 'Shining Online' and for making an impact and being an inspiration to women in the UK.

Yvette has been featured on international radio programmes, been in *Yoga* magazine, *High Spirit* magazine, and shared her message on stage with world-renowned names such as Bruce Cryer, Ali Brown and Dr Joanna Martin and well-known names like Bob Proctor, Bruce Lipton and Andy Dooley.

Lisa Hammond is the creator of Universal Heart Ascension and Co-founder of EAM. Having worked for more than 20 years as a therapist, coach and healer, empowering those who are ready to change their lives to shift their frequency.

Lisa has trained with industry leaders such as Anne Jirsch, Penny Horsburgh and Yvette Taylor in Future Life Progression and Past Life Regression, Reiki Master and Teaching, Egyptian Alchemy Healing and is a Visionary Life Stylist. She was one of the first 20 EAM mentors in the world. She has spoken on stage in front of thousands of people at live events.

Winner of global entrepreneurial awards for innovation, she has regularly featured in national and industry magazines and worked with high-profile celebrities. With a background in global travel, international event management, business sales strategy and hotel management, she has led global teams in creating highly successful and profitable businesses.

She's a loving mummy, and an empathic, positive, outgoing and empowering person to be around, always diplomatic and available to listen to what needs to be heard with an open heart. She is able to clearly help you find what others will not see.

Both Yvette and Lisa are entrepreneurs and change-makers by heart; they are huge advocates for change and shifting the world to a new paradigm.

YVETTE TAYLOR

WITH LISA HAMMOND

THE
ENERGY
ALIGNMENT
METHOD

LET GO OF THE PAST, FREE YOURSELF FROM SELF-SABOTAGE AND ATTRACT THE LIFE YOU WANT

WELBECK
BALANCE

A Trigger Book
Published by Welbeck Balance
An imprint of Welbeck Publishing Group
20 Mortimer Street
London W1T 3JW

First published by Welbeck Balance in 2021

A CIP catalogue record for this book is available from the British Library

ISBN – 9781789562477

Cover Design by Steve Williams Creative
Typeset by JCS Publishing Services Ltd
Printed in Great Britain by CPI Group (UK) Ltd,
Croydon CRO 4YY

10 9 8 7 6 5 4 3 2 1

www.welbeckpublishing.com

To all those who know there is something more.
Who are searching for the answers to life.
Who want to resolve world situations.
Who are ready to find their way home.
Back to themselves. Back to love. Back to alignment.
This book is dedicated to you.

FOREWORD

This book is a gift to every person who has the privilege of learning and applying its practical wisdom to create lives of freedom, health, wholeness, fulfillment and joy. As you will learn in the pages ahead, recent discoveries in neuroscience have confirmed ancient wisdom from thousands of years ago, turning much of our modern-day 'conventional wisdom' upside down. This book is a brilliant blend of the latest cognitive, cardiovascular, epigenetic and quantum science, with the uber-practical and transformational Energy Alignment Method® (EAM) process.

In 1990 I had the privilege of being invited into the founding leadership team of HeartMath (a leading organization looking at the connection between the heart and the mind) by founder Doc Childre. Over the next two decades, along with colleagues at Stanford University and other major research centres around the world, we developed foundational work in the science of personal transformation. Later, as CEO of HeartMath, I worked with clients such as the NHS, Shell, Unilever, the Dutch National Police and many others spanning four continents, testing our tools and methodologies in the real world.

Through these experiences and through my personal health journey and eventual renaissance, I have come to understand that every human being is born with a unique creative power that can unfold and flower throughout every aspect of life. Few of us have ever had a system to awaken this hidden, unique potential, much less give birth to it.

Based on thousands of years of insight from Eastern medicine traditions, and grounded in the reality of humanity in pain, the concepts outlined here are well-tested and studied with 50,000+ participants over the past few years. In addition, they are closely aligned with the latest breakthroughs from the heart coherence work pioneered by the HeartMath Institute, and the powerful discoveries of visionary researchers such as Dr Bruce Lipton and Dr Joe Dispenza.

In the middle of February 2020, before the world realized we were just weeks away from a global pandemic that would change everything, I was visiting Los Angeles with my dear friend and colleague Steinar Ditlefsen.

It had been a very impactful week for me already, having just completed six remarkable days at one of Dr Dispenza's powerful week-long advanced retreats in the desert near Palm Springs. Sadly, I had to leave the retreat early in order to attend the memorial service of my brother who had passed away just weeks earlier.

After the service, I flew back to LA to meet the group of 15 European transformational teachers Steinar had brought to the US to meet with various spiritual leaders. The visit seemed like the perfect way to complete a deeply moving and transformational week.

Of the many shining stars within the group I would meet that week, one that I connected with profoundly was Yvette Taylor. There is a clarity, a balance, a care, and a playfulness in Yvette that I deeply appreciate. She is my 'sister from another mister'. Soul family for sure.

I had heard of the Energy Alignment Method months earlier at an event in Cannes, France, where a number of the attendees referred quite proudly to being 'EAM mentors'. I was intrigued.

Upon meeting Yvette in LA and seeing her teach over this last year, I have seen the power of this system you are about to learn. EAM is indeed life-changing because it works directly at the level of our energy itself.

These methods are definitely not band-aids to be placed over hurt or pain. They are deeply transformative tools which have changed the lives of thousands of individuals already. As Yvette clearly expresses, 'The purpose of everything within EAM is to align your whole energy field and raise your frequency.'

As someone who deeply values rigorous science in the pursuit of spiritual and personal growth, I am impressed that this book is very smart without being academic. It strikes a comfortable balance in being scientific enough for the layperson without being snooze-worthy or pseudo-scientific. In fact, it is more robust in its scientific clarity and precision than similar books I've read. Yet it remains sufficiently spiritual and inspiring that you will want to expand your perspective and understanding of energy.

In the pages to come, leave any worries or skepticism behind and allow yourself to experience a new world opening up inside of you. You will be gently and confidently guided to explore the subconscious patterns, resistances, and energetic beliefs that have been keeping you from living the life of your dreams.

You will emerge new.

Stronger. Confident. Hopeful. Empowered.

It's a privilege and an honour to introduce you to this marvellous work.

Bruce Cryer
President, The Graduate Institute
Founder, Renaissance Human
Adjunct Faculty, Stanford University

CONTENTS

INTRODUCTION

You hold the answer to *it* and everything you're searching for already.

For millennia, we've tried to define *it*, to discover the source and meaning of life itself. We've asked ourselves, 'Why am I here?', 'What is the purpose of life?', 'How does it work?'

We've created stories, philosophies, rituals and religions to describe *it*. We've shared our understanding of *it* over campfires, in books, on podiums and street corners.

We've started and ended wars, invaded and recaptured lands, created and lost many civilizations because of *it*. *It* has been used to control, manipulate and instil fear. *It* has been used to spread love, peace, harmony and create freedom.

Whichever community, country, ethnicity or religion we come from, we have our perspective of *it* too, and this has been passed through the generations.

What if the answer to *it* has been there all along? What if we'd simply let go of what we think we know to see what *it* really is.

The 'it' we're describing is the invisible subtle force holding the web of life together. The overarching, all-seeing, all-knowing energy that drives and creates everything. The 'unknown', mystical, inexplicable element of our existence. We may call it Qi, God, source, energy, vibration, light, lightforce, prana, nature, love, the field, magnetism, force, universal presence, potential energy or any number of other labels. Choose whichever works for you, as all of them describe this.

Nikola Tesla said, *'If you want to find the secrets of the universe, think in terms of energy, frequency and vibration.'*

If this is true, what if the answer to understanding yourself, letting go of your past, freeing yourself from sabotage and attracting the life you deserve lived there, too? Now modern sciences such as quantum physics are proving the subtle understandings of life known by many ancient cultures.

When you understand that **everything is energy**, meaning you are energy, as is everything inside and outside of you, you can enter a field of unseen resources already available for you to change your life right now.

This understanding is key to the Energy Alignment Method® (EAM), and will unfold as you continue to read this book.

Energy connects everything seen and unseen in our universe. Energy never dies, it only transforms. As humans, we must remember we are connected to it all.

Think of the vast universe full of galaxies, solar systems and planets. Our beautiful earth, Gaia, creating life for 4.5 billion years. The incredible ecosystems, species, wildlife, sea life, humbling mountains, endless plains, never-ending varieties of flora and fauna. Imagine the cumulative years of life that existed before us. That energy still exists. It never died, it was reborn, transformed. It creates and sustains us.

We're made from the same force that created all of this. Do you see how powerful we already are? You can manifest, direct and transform *anything* when working with energy.

It can be easy to get wrapped up in our own life, thinking that we're individual or separate. The truth is, you're part of something far greater: we're *all* connected. This is more than some spiritual nicety; it's also a scientific truth. By creating energetic changes in yourself with EAM, you'll change your life and those around you. The effects of which will ripple out far beyond and into the world, contributing to the change in humanity.

Please know you're reading this book for a reason, the universe is pointing you in the right direction – EAM is the missing piece of the puzzle.

What Is EAM?

The Energy Alignment Method is an internationally recognized complementary therapy. It's a simple yet transformational five-step self-help technique designed to shift energy, thoughts and emotions so you can change what you see, feel or experience in your life.

It's been described as a bridge between science and spirituality. Founded on more than 20+ years of working with energy medicine, Law of Attraction and traditional Chinese medicine, EAM is a blend of kinesiology, neuro-scientific research, neuro-linguistic programming (NLP), positive psychology and Eastern practices. However, EAM is more than just another mindset tool – with it, there's no need to regurgitate the past or dig up memories. And it's more than a manifesting tool – it's a way of life. Very simply, these are the five steps:

Step 1 – You Ask	Ask your subconscious a question
Step 2 – You Move	Your energy field will respond
Step 3 – You Experience	Understand how it affects your energy
Step 4 – You Transform	Release what stands in your way
Step 5 – You Manifest	Create a new thought, belief, pattern, emotion or experience

There is clearly more to it than this – we'll explain it further and show you how to put it into practice later in the book. By combining these concepts, EAM allows you to be in 'flow' – that harmonious state where you feel totally in tune with life, 'in the zone' and trust everything is working out for you. By reading this book and doing the exercises, we will show you how to transform your energy, create positive thinking, shift feelings and change your outlook.

We've All Been There

We've all experienced being out of flow or in resistance. Those days when you wake up and your mind is filled with repetitive thoughts, consumed with negativity you're unable to shake, perhaps carrying heavy emotional pain, hidden memories or traumatic experiences from the past. Or we're stuck in a loop, living with stress, anxiety and overwhelm for so long that we have no idea what could lie beyond it. Also, if our physical body is limited by illness, this stops us from having an active carefree life.

There are many ways being out of flow shows up – being stuck in the past; staying in painful unstable relationships; physical pain or tiredness; confusion or indecision; failure; procrastination; obsession; harsh self-judgement; feeling unworthy or not good enough; feelings of guilt; blame; shame; jealousy; overwhelm; stress or anxiety; chronic debt; poor boundaries; confusion; indecision. Shall we go on?!! The good news is that all of them are expressions of what's happening to you energetically.

Now you may be thinking, *'I've been all of these.'* We all have at one time or another, sometimes many times a day. Please know you're never alone. Millions of us are searching for a new way of being, to feel happier, healthier and more in control of our lives in a fast-moving and chaotic world. We were simply never designed to live this way.

My search began because I wanted to change my life. This quickly evolved into a passion, with me reading every self-help book and qualifying in every relevant field, yet still feeling frustrated at conflicting answers, concepts and rules. Trying to find the 'secret' that no one would clearly say out loud. What was it? We now know this is flow.

Create More Flow

Ever had those moments when you feel in tune with life around you, everything seems effortless and you feel on top of the world? It's often known as 'being in the zone', in alignment, receptive, in sync or coherence. All these terms describe an easily achievable powerful natural state of flow. We'll use them interchangeably throughout this book.

Physically and scientifically, flow creates measurable changes throughout your physical body. It influences signals sent to and from your brain, changes heart waves, hormone levels and release of endorphins. This resolves stress and anxiety, and promotes healing, feelings of calm, happiness and love. It feels like bliss!

Through applying EAM, you're able to change your resistant or negative energy, thoughts and emotions, then choose to create the receptive or flow state around any situation. Imagine having the power to find and remove hidden issues and create a sense of inner strength that serves you to achieve your dreams and turn them into your reality!

In this book we'll look at how the three flows of energy influence your life, and understand the science behind this.

We'll gain a deeper understanding of your energy system and how it helps or holds you back; we'll explore the key concepts and Five Steps of EAM so you can use them everyday and successfully put them into practice; and we'll learn a ten-step journey to change your life and see how you can change the world along the way.

The Birth of EAM

There is no denying that everything in our life experience affects our energy. It's the energetic, emotional and mental impact of this that often sends us on the search to change our life. Let me share a story with you.

Frozen still, this 12-year-old girl was sh** scared, she felt small, powerless and hopeless. As her face pushed up against the cold hard bathtub, squeezed down, unable to move, trying to push this heavy weight on top of her away. This stranger had one hand on her neck, as she stared at the knife in the other, silently holding a scream inside, desperate to call out. She daren't breathe, speak or make a sound; she gave in, laid still and let him finish.

At that moment, she made an unconscious decision to trust no one, believing no one could protect her and that she had to do life on her own. Holding onto these secrets, petrified she'd get into trouble if she told her parents or anyone, she bottled it up inside, becoming angry at life. Every ounce of her spark and childhood was gone; she was in survival mode. Up to this point, life had been less than perfect, living in fear of dad staggering in smelling of beer, starting yet another fight. And then surviving four years battling a life-threatening illness – it all became too much.

Turning to alcohol, drugs and partying to temporarily numb the pain, she found relief and solace in setting fire to herself, stubbing cigarettes on her arms and legs, cutting herself or punching herself in the face. While none of this worked, it was the only way she knew to control how she felt inside.

After a few years, she began to think there had to be more to life. The universe delivered the first step when she saw the film *The Secret*. Then she began to search, consuming every book, video, audio on the topic and talking to every psychic, always asking the same question, '**HOW DO I CHANGE MY LIFE?**' Eventually, she got sick of hearing people say,

'Just let it go'
'Just be more positive'
'You get what you think about'
'You're not what happened to you'
'Just forget about it'
'Just focus on your future'

'*Yes*,' she thought, as she silently screamed inside, '*I know you're right, but HOW?*' When you're so in pain, consumed by your story, the past negativity, stuck in frustration, living in chaos, plagued by memories every time you close your eyes, what on earth do you do? You step into the world of energy.

That brave little girl taught me a lot. With hindsight, it all makes sense. Everything led to this point in life. Without it, EAM would never exist. I would never have been so driven to change my life and explore the world of energy. Never in a million years did *that* little girl believe she'd be sharing *this* with you now. Along the way I've discovered so many answers, which we will unfold inside this book. These I have to share with you now.

- EVERYTHING IS ENERGY
Everything we experience is *all just energy*. This includes you, and you need to know how to shift and change your energy state at will.

- THE REASON WHY WE KEEP SEARCHING
We've been looking in the wrong place. It's never outside, it's always within. We're all different – our journey, lessons and interpretations. Our uniqueness means the answer to changing *your* life can only lie with you.

- YOU HAVE THE POWER TO CHANGE YOUR LIFE
When you tap into your energy field, you can change anything in your life. Whatever happened in your past, you can let go. This is never to diminish your experience. It's simply to inspire you that there *is* a way to change it and let it go.

ALL of these things are exactly what we want to show you can change with EAM. You may have heard this all before, this time please hear it, EAM is empowering so many people just like you. Listen to the 50,000+ people (and growing) who've used it to change their life. Or read our research studies of 17,000+ people with amazing results. Now it's an internationally recognized complementary therapy, too.

There are no empty promises to manifest your dreams in 15 seconds or become a millionaire in the next 45 minutes. If you want a 'quick fix', please close this book. If you're ready for lifelong transformations and to learn a simple five-step process you can use to change anything, then read on.

Now, along the way I met a very incredible lady, who I feel so blessed to know – Lisa Hammond. Over the last few years, we've been sharing EAM and changing the lives of those who are putting it into practice. Let me hand you over to meet Lisa here, to continue our story.

Lisa: My life began with me having older parents – as having more children was impossible at their age, I grew up with a lot of time on my own. Fascinated by *Star Wars* and anything out of this world, I experienced energy very early on. Before the age of ten, I was leading friends through meditations and stories into other worlds! I remember writing '*I know I AM here for something but don't know what it is*'. Downloading and 'giving' people information felt natural for me, I knew no different.

However, being surrounded by some family members with mental health issues left me feeling anxious and walking on eggshells. Here, my intuition truly kicked in – being able to read others was a gift for navigating my way through.

I became an 'activator', meaning I could attract certain relationships or people to support and help others on their way. I became everyone's 'go to'. If I reached out for support myself, it was rarely met with the same response, so I became more insular and began searching deeper inside.

It was only when a series of events began to shatter my reality – I lost my father quite suddenly to pancreatic cancer – my life changed and my understanding of energy and intuition really opened up again. Helping my father spiritually transition, I realized so much of me had gone with him. This is when I started to learn about the work of a soul midwife and about soul retrieval. But the main element was how we all were connected in other dimensions. I knew how old my soul was and what role I was here to play – to be a light, guide and wayshower.

The year after this, my son was born. As a busy mum, running my own business, I'd wait until he was asleep before starting work at 1am in the morning. The universe, having had enough and knowing I wasn't doing the work I was meant for, pulled the rug – a huge £million deal went bust and the business crumbled, creating a cascade of losing my home, business, relationship and accumulating a mountain of debt.

This was the turning point to open my life up to service. I knew it was about moving in another direction, where I could see the difference I was here for. It was time to be self-reliant, to love myself and be my own rock in the transformation to the new paradigm.

Even though my life at this time had been the darkest I'd experienced, I learned to trust there is always something bigger at play even when you've no idea what it is. I came to know that when someone has passed, they're still constantly with you, giving you signs and making things happen. Also, I knew that to change our lives the answers are within.

This was my time of transformation, like a phoenix rising out of the ashes. Then, out of nowhere, Yvette appeared online, sharing a short seven-day online programme called Fear to Love. We booked in a call, which became an interview. It was as if the universe kicked me, and I had an overwhelming moment to say, '*I know I AM meant to help you.*'

From there, the rest is history. Over this journey we've been honoured to share EAM with thousands of people around the world, we've got a growing team and network of mentors. It has been an expansive, exciting and scary journey, that's for sure. Over these last few years since using EAM my intuitive abilities and senses have expanded at a rapid rate. Now, I get to integrate my spiritual side into the business world and change thousands of lives whilst we're at it.

Now, together we want to share with you one of the most powerful transformational tools we've ever, ever used – EAM – and show you how you can use it too.

Our mission is to empower a global wave of people to step into their power, to play our part in changing the planet, by sharing EAM, shifting energy and raising the vibrational frequency of billions of people. It's about bringing forward the change from living in the old paradigm of fear, blame and shame to the new paradigm of love, connection and collaboration. This is about bringing in a new way of living: one that is empowering, healthy and sustainable for every being on this planet – plants, animals and humans alike. EAM is way of life.

Get Ready to Read!

Together, we'll take you on a journey in this book. There'll be many different topics introduced based on science or facts. Others may be theories, concepts and observations. The truth is, we're all using our limited language to explain something intangible. We openly invite you to be sceptical and, at the same time, to open your mind beyond what you know. Take what resonates with you, and follow the work for yourself to prove these ideas by changing these aspects in your life. That is the only truth we ever need.

While you may be tempted to jump straight to the 'Five Steps', the chapters before will give you a level of understanding about yourself, your physiology, psychology and energetic systems, and how they all contribute to your success. While you can use the Five Steps of EAM without it, a new level of insight about yourself is always profound.

Get yourself a journal to make notes of the ideas and to complete the exercises in this book. This is going to be a co-creative experience. You're not alone. Come and meet the other people on this journey at www.energyalignment method.com/join-the-community.

The simple truth is your success is based on your commitment. To change your life, you have to make space for it. Our wish is that you'll finish this book more empowered than you were at the beginning, with a greater understanding of the power you have, and knowing your body, mind and energy in a whole new way. We hope that you'll have put the Five Steps of EAM into practice, knowing how to apply them in your life, every day.

Here is our other promise – we'll keep it real and have some fun along the way! Now it's time for us to truly begin. Are you ready?

PART ONE

IT'S ALL ABOUT ENERGY

Chapter 1

ELECTROMAGNETIC ENERGY

BOOM. From nothing it all exists. An explosion of energy that created life itself. No matter which ancient mythology or religious philosophy you refer to, they all talk about the beginning of life or birth of creation where everything came into form from nothing. To date, no one has been able to explain or fully agree on the origins of our universe, yet we often refer to this time as the Big Bang!

In this chapter, we'll talk about energy from a scientific perspective. You'll understand some key energy principles that apply to everything in your life. Our universe is made of structures so huge they're beyond comprehension to particles so tiny they're impossible to imagine. Extensive research into many branches of science deepens our understanding. They may focus on different areas – geology, astronomy, chemistry, maths, physics, to name a few – but what unites them is the exploration of energy in all its forms. Technically, energy can be broken down into kinetic, chemical, thermal or potential energy. For our purposes we'll refer to them all as electromagnetic energy.

When we look at all life on earth, everything requires some form of energy in order to survive. When no energy sources are present, life will die. The majority of life requires light in order to grow – think of plants growing toward the sun, photosynthesis producing oxygen, and algae blooming in our oceans. The same applies to us, too. We need light in order to thrive, grow and expand.

The physics taught in school focuses on life at a macroscopic scale – the world we observe. Yet it's at the tiniest, unimaginable levels that energy becomes interesting. For this, we need to dip into quantum mechanics – the study of matter as atomic and subatomic particles. It's here that energy theory will help to explain the concepts and workings of EAM.

In addition to Western scientific concepts and theories, we also draw on Eastern traditions when looking at the understanding of energy in the macro- and microcosm. Here, energy called 'Qi' or 'prana' interacts with our environment and flows through our meridians, chakras and aura – we'll explore this more in Chapter 4. First, let's look at electromagnetic energy.

What Is Electromagnetic Energy?

Electromagnetic energy is a term used to describe electrical or magnetic waves that travel through space. They're all light waves, meaning all energy is, in fact, light. These electromagnetic waves range from gamma rays and X-rays, through UV light, visible light, infrared light, microwaves and radio waves. They're classified according to their frequency, each with a different use in our everyday lives.

When talking about energy, you'll often hear terms such as wavelength, frequency and vibration, which all describe the actions or behaviour of the energy. If we imagine a ball bouncing along the ground, wavelength would describe the distance between each bounce; the length from one bounce point to another.

Frequency or vibration would describe how many times that ball bounced within a given distance. Frequency is usually measured in units known as hertz. So, frequency is

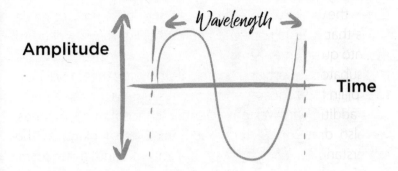

simply the number of vibrations within a particular amount of time or distance.

We call the faster electromagnetic wave energies 'higher vibrations', because they're short, fast and light. The longer waves, which are slower, heavier and denser in energy, are called 'lower vibrations'.

We all experience the world vibrationally. It's important to understand the vast range of energy, in all its forms, which influences and impacts us each and every day.

Everything is energy, vibrating at different levels or frequencies. Everything is constantly moving, even when it may appear to be static. The graphic on the next page represents the different vibrations of electromagnetic energy all around us.

Everything is energy, simply vibrating at different frequencies.

On the left, are gamma rays, which are short waves of energy vibrating at a very fast, high pace. The shorter the wavelength, the greater the energy produced. These rays

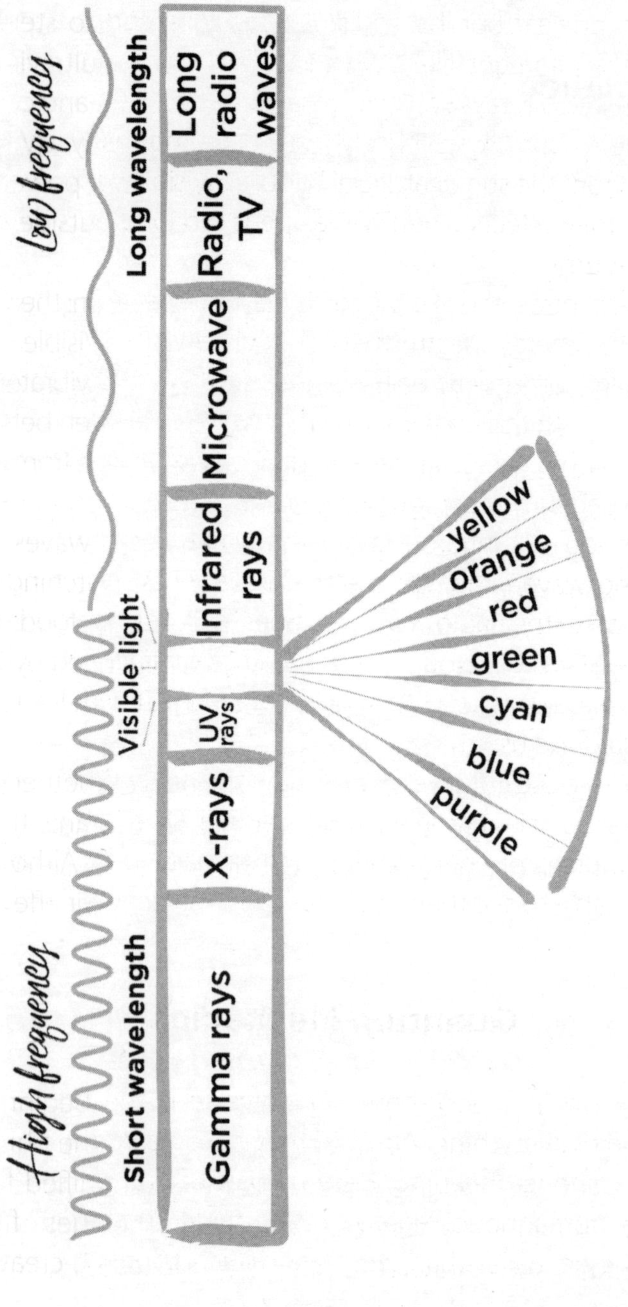

Low frequency

Long wavelength

Long radio waves

Radio, TV

Microwave

Infrared rays

Visible light

UV rays

X-rays

Gamma rays

Short wavelength

High frequency

yellow
orange
red
green
cyan
blue
purple

Electromagnetic spectrum

affect our energy field and can cause us great harm. They're used in nuclear bombs, to kill cancer cells, and to sterilize hospital equipment. Next, we find X-rays and UV (ultraviolet) rays. We know X-rays can give us radiation sickness and cause damage to our physical body if we have too many. UV rays radiate from the sun or artificial lights – invisible yet powerful, we see their effects when we've spent too long outside and get sunburnt.

In the centre is the expanded visible light spectrum: the only part of the energy spectrum we're visually aware of. Visible light is also electromagnetic energy and everything that vibrates or resonates with this frequency is what we see. We often behave as if only what we see and feel exists. Yet, we can see from this whole spectrum of energy that is far from the truth.

Next you see infrared rays, microwaves, radio waves, TV, and long wave radio. We use them every day, watching TV, listening to the radio, using phones or cooking food. We forget that we're surrounded, affected and influenced by this energy, everyday like a fish in water. We interact with it – it's in and all around us.

When we use EAM we're working with energy. Whether you look at it as 'scientific' energy or 'spiritual' Qi or prana, these unseen forces of energy influence our daily lives. Although we're unable to see them with our eyes, we feel their effects.

Quantum Mechanics

We learned in school how our universe is the beginning and end of everything. And you may have heard the phrase, 'we are all one', meaning we're *all* part of one unified field of electromagnetic energy. Everything emerges from something smaller than electrons, which connect, creating this one invisible field. Look at it this way, our body is made of bone, tissue and blood. These elements are made of cells, which are made from organelles, made from proteins, made of amino acids, which are made of atoms. Atoms are made of protons, neutrons and electrons. Electrons are made from the electron field. So, what on earth is that field made of? Potential energy!

This brings us to the world of quantum mechanics, or quantum physics, the branch of physics relating to the microcosmic world, much smaller than we see with a normal microscope. It's a set of theories explaining what happens at the atomic and subatomic levels of our life experience. Quantum mechanics is often described as the science of possibility, which is such a profound and exciting concept. Science has shown that at the quantum level everything is energy. In that nothingness or potential energy comes everything. Everything you believe to be possible.

The Power of the Observer

One of the most exciting experiments in the world of quantum physics is the 'double slit' test. This incredible experiment proves that everything around us exists by being experienced by YOU or ME, the observer!

In essence, the experiment shows that tiny electrons 'decide' what to do in response to being observed. When energy goes unobserved it behaves like a wave of water; when observed, it behaves like a ball.

What does this mean to us? Electrons are affected and behave differently, depending on observation, when a mind is present. Energy *only* appears as matter when it's being observed. Deep, right? Yes! Empowering? ABSOLUTELY! It means that ALL of reality is actually one big field of energy with potential for anything, because how we observe it changes its (and our) reality.

Why is this important to you? This experiment shows that *we* shape our reality, through vibration of energy, thoughts, words, emotions and our conscious and subconscious awareness. This means we can change what we see by changing our vibration, which shifts perception, in turn altering our reality. It also shows that we can choose to define what we see through the power of intention. From a quantum perspective, that's what we're doing with EAM.

There are differing schools of thought on quantum physics. Some believe that we're part of multiple realities or parallel universes. The 'many worlds' theory holds that many universes are working at the same time, where every possible event is occurring. For whatever reason, our awareness only sees one. Alternatively, the 'Copenhagen interpretation' theorizes that we interact with waves of energy and create our experience from an infinite number of possibilities.

It's us observing potential energy that creates 'reality'.

Whichever theory you feel aligned to, it's us *observing* potential energy that allows this to become the physical form, meaning we manifest it into 'reality'. This raises the bigger question of which 'reality' is true? This is a key part of the energy puzzle, remember that we have this power. We create our life through our perception. You'll see how learning to shift and change your frequency in the unified field of electromagnetic energy can alter the life or reality you see. In EAM and other practices, this is known as manifesting.

The Movements of Energy

Scientific studies by Bruce Lipton in his work *The Biology of Belief* (Hay House, 2015) have shown that cells will move in one of three directions depending on what's present in their environment. They'll move toward or forward for positive signals such as food, they'll remain stationary or stuck when something is neutral or unmotivating, and they'll move away or shut down and protect themselves from dangers, threats or poisons in their environment. This means that energy is moving in one of three states: from one place to another, stationary, or moving in the opposite direction. This body of work was a key foundational concept in the formation of EAM, and is especially important when talking about our own vibrational field and perceptions later on.

In physics terms, 'flow' means moving steadily and continuously without stopping. 'Resistance' is a force that stops progression of something or makes it slower, or is the degree to which something prevents the flow of an electrical current. 'Reversal' is the act of changing, or making something change, to its opposite. You'll find these terms used in physics in relation to flows of energy. We also use them in terms of energy psychology and you'll see how they apply to your life in Chapter 3.

An electromagnetic field (also EMF or EM field) is a physical field produced by electrically charged objects, which are charged by electrons. As the name suggests, this field is both *electric*, meaning it holds a charge, and *magnetic* meaning it attracts things of a like vibration back to it. By its very nature of being electric and magnetic, the electrons involved affect other electrons in their vicinity. When looking at energy in transmission systems, such as radio waves, there's something in the signal itself known as the carrier wave. It's a waveform with the purpose of transmitting information carried by the electromagnetic elements of the wave.

When you think about the structure of energy, imagine it in three components: the electricity, the magnetism and the message. Firstly, the flow of electricity, or power source or battery, travels up and down. This represents the two extremes of energy, yin and yang, or positive and negative. Secondly, the magnetic element of energy is flowing left and right, attracting and drawing in or pushing elements away from us – this creates our horizontal experience in life. The third component is the 'message', which is sent via a carrier wave out into the world. You'll see later that our own energy system is structured in the same way.

This flow of electromagnetic energy affects everything, whether we're talking about a tiny cell in our body or the environment around us. They're all connected. Everything within and around us is energy in motion and we're influenced by it all.

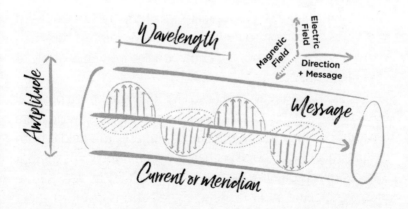

Electromagnetic wavelength structure and message transmission

Interpreting Vibration

We have five physical senses – sight, sound, touch, smell and taste – and each one has a specific role and is a translator of a particular type of electromagnetic vibration. For example, eyes receive and interpret a particular range of the spectrum known as visible light waves. Ears interpret mechanical energy as sound waves. Skin interprets a range of pressure, temperature and pain. Our senses of taste and smell offer more interpretations of molecules that lock into receptors and send signals via our nervous system. In its own way, each is an indicator of vibration.

Other animals also experience different vibrational ranges of energy. For example, a dog has a greater perception of the range of smell and sound than we do, and some animals can see in the dark using infrared waves. It's possible for biology to perceive a large range of electromagnetic frequencies, so while many animals are highly tuned and capable, most human bodies are not yet adapted to do so.

We're built to interpret vibration in all its forms.

In order to process all of that information coming at us, our brain and body has to filter it. This happens in a part of the brain known as the thalamus. If we were unable to filter out all that extra information and noise, we'd go mad! Our senses pick up far more information from the electromagnetic field than we consciously perceive in our reality. What you 'see' is an inaccurate or incomplete picture. It's your interpretation of the energetic information around you, which was filtered through the lenses of your own experiences. We'll explore a little more of how this happens.

The good news is we're built to interpret vibration of energy in all its different forms. So it stands to reason that we're also reading other energy in the electron field, even if we're yet to learn that is what we're interpreting. By understanding how your system works and using the Energy Alignment Method, we can change what we see and experience. This gives a sense of empowerment – we see how to change ourselves and our environment for the better and attract the life we deserve.

Chapter Two

THE THREE FLOWS OF ENERGY

In the previous chapter we explored the three movements of energy: forward, stationary or away from (see p. 22). These three flows of energy are a key concept in EAM. Understanding them will simplify everything with EAM and allow you to embrace what we're really doing because these three flows apply to everything in life. Whatever you experience, it will be in one of these three energetic states: receptive (in flow), resistance or reversal. In this chapter, we'll explore this further and examine how they impact different areas of our life experience. First, let's take a look at how we experience life on multiple levels simultaneously.

We're multidimensional, we experience life on different levels.

The Seven Levels of Life Experience

As human beings, we're multidimensional, meaning we experience life in many ways on different levels. All of them are differing expressions of electromagnetic energy on a micro- or macrocosmic level, all coexisting, influencing the other, and collectively making up our life experience. There are seven key levels for us to explore:

THE THREE FLOWS OF ENERGY

1. Spiritual Energy
This is best described as source or potential energy, the 'unknown' or mystical foundation of the universe itself. People may refer to spirit, energy or acts of God, astrology and the movements of planets. It also refers to what happens in the unknown depths of our own energy system.

2. Electromagnetic Energy
This represents quantum and electromagnetic energy in our inner and outer worlds. This is what mainstream science is able to track, measure and examine. As well as in ourselves or in technology, think of it in terms of solar flares, magnetic pulses and shifts in the earth's biofield, as well as our interaction with radio waves, gamma rays, X-rays and all of the energies we live with today.

3. Cellular or DNA Energy
We experience life at a cellular or DNA level of ourselves. Remember, we're a massive community of organisms, not just one single human body. There's a wealth of life experience happening on a tiny level, every second, without our conscious awareness. Yet, we know when this energy is out of flow as it impacts physical health.

4. Material or Physical Elements
This refers to our physical body and the material-based physical elements of life, such as objects and people. It's the aspect we consider 'real' because it's what we see and, therefore, give most conscious awareness to.

5. Emotional Experiences
What we *feel is* a key aspect that determines life experience. We'll remember how we *felt* in a situation more than the physical details or what was said.

6. Psychological Constructs
This level of thoughts, memories, beliefs and patterns makes up our thinking or logical mind. These mental constructs influence our life through our interpretation of information in our environment.

7. Mass Consciousness
Of course, we're also part of a collective, mass or a global consciousness – the one mind. Energetically, this is co-created through communication, what we think, feel, see and have experienced in our shared society.

It's important to remember that we experience life on multiple levels, all of them connected. Coming from the one unified field, what we experience on one level will also be expressed in others. In Eastern philosophy, it's often shown as 'what is outside is what is within'. Again, this is a key concept when thinking of our own life experience and applying EAM.

Let's take a brief look at what each of these areas may look like when in one of the three energy states or flows, and how using EAM can create shifts and transformations in every area of life.

Remember, everything is electromagnetic energy, including us. Therefore, energy is either moving in one direction from one place to another (receptive or 'in flow'), stationary (resistant), or moving in the opposite direction (reversal). These three flows of energy are ones you'll see us refer to time and time again in this book. We want to take the time to explore them so you know how they're created and how they may show up in everyday life.

Three Flows of Energy

⟵ ⟷ ⟶

Reversal   **Resistance**   **Receptive**

Reversal

The term 'reversal' is often used to describe the act of changing or making something change to its opposite. In energy psychology, reversals describe energy flowing in the opposite direction to what it would normally be – like a shock or disruption in our energy field. It can become literally stuck or frozen, or so much so it will reverse the flow. Energy reversals prevent the free flow of positive Qi around that part of your life, body or a particular subject.

They can be created by things in our environment, such as wifi, 5G or even people. More commonly, energy reversals are created in situations where we've no 'normal' coping mechanism, or we're shocked or surprised by the event or outcome. The reversal is then formed by the decisions, choices and experiences that are connecting in our energy field.

If we could see a reversal in your energy, imagine it looks like a dark swirling circle, fracture, crack or break in your vibration, like a broken plate that has been glued back together. Often, these broken pieces have rewired parts of your energy – thoughts, beliefs, emotions – and made neurological connections in your brain with incorrect interpretations of information. This is why we sometimes see seemingly irrational behaviour.

29

These reversals can cause pieces of your energy to separate like small Russian dolls, and part of you stays that age, becoming stuck in that experience. When faced with the same or similar situation, you react in the same way. While you still have energy reversals, you'll recreate similar scenarios in your life, because that's what's active in your field. You've probably seen a reversal in action (or had one yourself!) when you see an adult suddenly behaving like a child.

These energy reversals are powerful. *Everyone* has them, on all kinds of subjects, and often multiple reversals on some. Ironically, they're designed to protect us and to keep us from danger, yet when it comes to energy psychology they're hidden gremlins.

Unless you address the reversed energy, it's almost impossible to change that area of your life, because energy is flowing *away from* instead of *toward* what you want. Every time you give energy to that subject, it pulls in the opposite direction. This is why our biggest challenges seem to get bigger the more attention we give them.

Unless you address reversed energy,
it's impossible to change your life.

In EAM, energy reversals are the root cause of stuck energy patterns, which never seem to shift. Addictions and repetitive states of living, such as being broke, doing work we hate or staying in unhappy relationships are examples of this. Reversals create beliefs, strong emotions and repeating habits or behaviours, which are ultimately self-sabotaging. Frequently, this is why some traditional forms of therapy or self-help may fail to work. If the reversal was never addressed energetically, or was only addressed on one level (for example, psychologically or with medication to numb its effects), it will continue to influence energetically, mentally and emotionally.

Using the sway (a key tool in the EAM process, which we'll explore shortly) we're able to identify what your energy reversals are, even on an unconscious level. You can discover when the energy reversal began, what the emotional, mental, physical or spiritual cause is, as well as how it's affecting your frequency. We then use the Five Steps of EAM to address this. When you do, you'll feel the transformation of your Qi into the flow state. Changing energy reversals are often our biggest breakthroughs, as all of the Qi previously stuck begins flowing toward what you want.

Physiologically, when a reversal is created it puts us into a state of shock. At that point, we make choices and decisions and energetically, mentally and emotionally connect them to seemingly disconnected events. This creates conflicts in our energy field. The situations that caused them are never usually very big or memorable. It was a shock to your vibrational field at the time. Conversely, if there have been big, catastrophic or tragic events, there'll most certainly be energy reversals (often multiple ones) connected. Within EAM, we explore energy reversals and resistances coming from many places. They can be passed down through generations in our family, in conception, your time in the womb, birth, this life, and other life experiences. For example, the thoughts, memories and emotions your mother experienced, and you perceived as a result, when carrying and giving birth to you, are imprinted in your energy. When using EAM, you can identify what these may be, as they will have influenced and shaped a lot of your life experience, and work to release any reversals.

Each of us experiences energy reversals differently, and different reversals will affect you differently too, depending which part of your energy system it has imprinted, what it's connected to, what the experience is and how it has affected the structures of your energy bodies. The reversal affects us when it's created, and any time we're reminded of that situation (consciously or unconsciously). This is made more difficult because when energy is 'broken', the parts it has been 'reconnected to' are often illogical, which is why our reactions with energy reversals can be highly irrational.

Reversals in our field can happen to varying degrees. For instance, someone jumping out from behind a tree can just make you jump or can trigger PTSD (post-traumatic stress disorder) if there has been a traumatic incident. That doesn't mean, however, that all reversals are PTSD. More frequently, it's in an area of life you feel unable to change or to understand why you're unable to change it. Often there's no 'significant' trauma to remember, so the cause remains elusive because there's no conscious 'event' connected. You may also have multiple reversals that contradict one another, because of this 'broken' connection of the information in your energy. Or you may be in resistance with one aspect of a situation and have a reversal on another.

Psychological studies have shown that from a neuroscience perspective these situations can create an experience of being frozen in time. When you're experiencing an energy reversal people often describe feeling numb about the subject, disorientated, unable to think or feel, or are overly emotional. This is literally what's happening in their aura or energy field and is a clear sign of a reversed energy state.

Here's an example of how a minor energy reversal may be created.

Four-year-old Lilly is at school painting a picture of home for her daddy. She loves to paint; he loves her paintings and always praises her for being so creative. Just as she picks up her brush to paint a tree by the front door, a little boy runs past, knocks over her paint pot and covers the floor in bright green paint. Her teacher missed seeing him run past. All she sees is the mess, and she shouts, *'No! Lilly, what are you doing? What an awful mess you've made.'*

Poor Lilly, who, moments ago, was happily painting her picture, jumps as she's shouted at. Right then, aged four, she makes an unconscious decision that painting is bad, that her work is rubbish and never to paint again because the teacher told her off. In that moment, her energy locks in the exact thoughts, words and emotions she's feeling and she now has a reversal about painting. The reality of it had nothing to do with the painting of the house. Later in life, Lilly stifles her art and creativity. She secretly longs to be a creative interior designer and architect, yet never pursues it because she believes that accessing her creativity is bad.

Although heart-breaking, sadly, this is a relatively mild example. Here, we have the other extreme.

Ivan lost his wife and child when his house was bombed in his war-stricken country. He managed to survive and rescue one child from the burning wreckage. In the disaster, he had to pull his burning child screaming from the building and helplessly watch as it collapsed with the rest of his family trapped inside. In that moment, an energy reversal was created as this event was such a shock to him and his energy. It was a situation he had never encountered before and had no coping strategy for. Afterwards, he's still locked in the event, replaying the scene and the sounds of his family screaming over and over in his head, agonizing over what he could have done differently.

These are often scenes we'd associate with psychologically recognized states of reversal, such as PTSD. Yet, we're all experiencing a range of reversals in every level of our life, all day every day.

Here are a few examples of how reversed energy affects the seven different levels of life experience:

- **Spiritual Energy** – There will be 'life lessons' or perceived obstacles to overcome, 'Russian doll' versions of ourselves separate, our energy becomes locked at that age, we get stuck repeating patterns, aura layers can collapse and chakras (see p. 75) can shut down.
- **Electromagnetic Energy** – Planets in retrograde, solar flares, interference from technology can cause reversals, resulting in incoherent heart patterns leading to deactivation of the frontal cortex of the brain and the hyper-activity of the limbic system, in particular, the amygdala.
- **Cellular or DNA Energy** – Reversals shut down the cell walls and prevent the exchange of fluids and foods. DNA genes which were previously inactive can be expressed due to the stressors found in our environment, causing onset of genetic health conditions.
- **Material or Physical Elements** – Chronic disease and serious or terminal illness. Constant 'fight or flight' in the body. Accidents, near misses and disasters.
- **Emotional Experiences** – High state of alert, debilitating fear, depression, stress anxiety and hopelessness.
- **Psychological Constructs** – Overly sensitive to the environment. Inappropriate mental or emotional responses, abnormal fears or phobias. Reliving of traumatic events, feeling disconnected and isolated.
- **Mass Consciousness** – A global mindset of fear, manipulation and control, people allowing themselves to be controlled, freezing, stopping their receptivity and believing they're powerless. Natural disasters, tsunamis, earthquakes.

You can deal with energy reversals in psychology and some energy healing practices, and, of course, with EAM. In our experience, until you address reversals energetically they'll pop up again because their imprint is still active in your energy field. By changing the energy system first, we see transformations expressed on all other levels of our life experience.

Letting go of an energy reversal is powerful. When we change reversals in our field with EAM, we get 'back in flow', we're able to access better choices, ideas and insight, and feel whole and complete.

Resistance

The dictionary defines resistance as, 'a force that acts to stop the progress of something, or make it slower, or the degree to which something prevents the flow of an electrical current through a circuit'. Resistance is also explained as 'a measurement of the difficulty encountered by a power source in forcing electric current through a circuit, and hence the amount of power dissipated in the circuit'. Notice the words in the definitions: 'stops progress', 'make it slower', 'prevents the flow', 'difficulty encountered', 'forcing', 'dissipated'. These concepts are exactly mirrored in the state of resistance, which we create in our lives and energy systems. When correlated to the movements of cells, this is almost stationary, or with little movement one way or another.

When receptive or in a flow state, energy will be travelling in one direction, moving forward with ease. When there's resistance it's because something creates a counter-flow. This results in a two-way movement of energy that creates a friction, tension or pull, which is what we experience as resistance. Energetically, this reflects in our life. Say you want to create something in your future, and there's a contradictory thought, belief, pattern or emotion holding you back. While it's active in your energy field, the two pull against each other, causing resistance.

If you were to see resistance in your energy field it would look like a fuzzy ball, creating distortion. Imagine a heaviness, darkness or lump. It would look constricted and uneven. It may be protective or solid.

Resistance is created in many ways, including thoughts, words, emotions, health, the food you eat, soap you wash with, other people's frequency, objects in the environment … The list is endless, because everything is energy in one of the three states. Resistance can also come from past or parallel lives, time in the womb or birth, throughout childhood and adult life. This creates a lot of possible places to explore with EAM to change resistance in your energy field. This is a journey – it will continue as you learn more about EAM, which we will introduce to you in this book.

What you experience as resistance is your heart and soul saying something is out of alignment. For example, you want a different job; your heart is urging you to pursue a new career doing something you enjoy. Yet, you hold a belief that you're unable to earn more money, and it's 'safer' to stay where you are because you have money coming in. There is a conflict between your thinking and feelings, which creates resistance, so you feel unable to move forward. This is a sign you need to do EAM to get back into alignment.

We've all experienced resistance. It's probably what brought you to this book. When something feels 'off', it feels like hard work and requires a lot of effort. Have you ever met someone you didn't like? What you sensed was their resistance, a mismatch between your energy fields. All the resistances or reversals we carry from the past show up in us, in our conversations, outlook and perception. This is how resistance expresses across all levels of our life experience.

- **Spiritual Energy** – Unable to move forward. Aura contracts, less Qi flows, chakras close and spin more slowly. Your head, heart and hara (see p. 81) send incongruent messages. Meridians (p. 73) get stuck. Life feels hard. You feel contracted and heavy.
- **Electromagnetic Energy** – Feelings of resistance are measured as lower, slower, heavier vibrations. Interference from technology.
- **Cellular or DNA Energy** – A decrease in fluid exchange and poor absorption into cells, they shut down and stop communicating as freely. DNA and gene expression can be impacted as they perceive stressors in the environment.
- **Material or Physical Elements** – Acute illnesses or short-term health conditions. High levels of cortisol and adrenaline impacting our physiology. Slips, trips, falls, knocks, dents, near misses.
- **Emotional Experiences** – Feeling blame, shame, anxiety, guilt, anger; feeling overwhelmed, frustration or jealousy.
- **Psychological Constructs** – Unable to think clearly, negative thoughts, unable to reason or recall information, decreased emotional stability, bad decisions and emotionally disconnected.
- **Mass Consciousness** – Separation, avoidance, unrest, riots, disconnection from humanity. Individual survival.

To get in alignment you have to first transform resistance. Many spiritual practices teach us to 'think positively'. However, unless we release the resistance or reversal first, we're working against conflicts in our energy.

What if you knew (like we do) the only thing preventing you from changing your life was the level of resistance or reversals you have in your energy? People say, *'No, it's because I have no money'*, or *'My partner is a pain in the ass'*, or *'You don't know what I've been through'*. We hear you. We get it. What if those beliefs were merely resistance, too? What will happen for you when you let them go?

While you hold resistance or reversals in your vibration, you'll repeat more of the same in your life. These are what stand in the way of changing your life every single time. It's why we've got such a passion to enable people to raise their vibration with EAM, to move past these energy states and shift into coherence. Once you do, watch how easily life starts to flow.

Receptive (in Flow)

The receptive mode is the state of flow, defined as 'something moving steadily and continuously without stopping'. As we talk about receptivity or flow, we're talking about all levels of our experience – energetic, physical, emotional and psychological. When in flow, we receive – we're in sync and can create change on all levels at once. You may have also heard flow called alignment. In EAM, it means the same thing; specifically, we use 'alignment' to mean that our key energy centres of head, heart, and hara are sending a congruent or harmonious message into the field.

Think of flow as an infinite source of potential energy, full of possibilities, love, happiness, positivity and abundance. It's the natural state of our energetic universe. This same energy state causes the universe itself to continually expand, change, develop and grow.

If you could see flow in your energy field, it would be beautifully even waves of energy, moving up and down like the tide, strong physical energy structures, open pulsating energy centres, shining light, waves of energy flowing around the body.

Within personal development, many people explore the state of flow in order to manifest external circumstances. It may be more money, power, love, wellness or any other life experience. Flow is about so much more than manifesting, it's *the* way of life. Everything in nature is in flow. It's external forces that cause this flow to cease.

> *Everything in nature is in flow, it's the way of life.*

Studies by the HeartMath Institute have shown the energy of flow moves in one consistent forward positive movement. When applied to your life, flow will allow you to be travelling in one positive direction toward everything you want. This is what EAM allows you to do.

Let's explore how the receptive or flow state expresses in the different levels of human experience we discussed earlier:

- **Spiritual Energy** – You vibrate at a higher, stronger frequency, attract more positive energy, manifest easily, have synchronistic experiences. It creates harmony, free flow of Qi and healing in your energy system. Your aura expands and strengthens; channels and meridians are wider, free-flowing; chakras are open. You receive insight, clarity, abundance and love. You're more in tune; intuition and psychic abilities are enhanced, your frequency sends stronger signals; you're more connected.

- **Electromagnetic Energy** – A more coherent heart rhythm pattern. This synchronizes communication throughout the body on a physical, mental, emotional and cellular level.
- **Cellular or DNA Energy** – Cells work and repair effectively, processing waste, allowing filtration, openly connecting and communicating, with normal healthy functions. DNA activates new expressions of what can occur with changes in physiology.
- **Material or Physical Elements** – Body in healing phase, changes in brain structure. More oxytocin, dopamine and endorphins in the body create euphoria.
- **Emotional Experiences** – Feel love, happiness, confidence, peace, joy, empowered and unstoppable. Sense of freedom and hope.
- **Psychological Constructs** – In 'the zone', 'on it', or 'present'. Shifts perception, improves mental and emotional stability. Greater clarity, focus and direction.
- **Mass Consciousness** – People come together, connect, love, support, collaborate, consider the wellbeing of themselves and others simultaneously, recognize and understand we are all one. Live in the new paradigm of abundance with enough resources available for everyone.

Aside from EAM, there are simple ways to be in flow. Go out in nature barefoot, get enough sleep, eat healthy well-balanced meals, go for a run, meditate, watch a comedy and laugh until your tummy hurts, dance like everyone's watching or go on a roller coaster ride. Really, any experience that snaps you out of daily habits and allows you to feel carefree, that is flow. When energy flow is receptive, everything feels effortless. You wake up feeling great, you find some money on the floor, someone buys you a coffee. You hear great news. You get a promotion and are taken out for dinner all in one day. The beauty is you can choose to be in that state any time you want, which is what we want to show you with EAM. First let's explore a little more about flow.

Chapter 3

THE FLOW STATE

We've explored flow state (receptive) in terms of EAM, however this is a phenomenon often used in places such as performance coaching, where it's described as the optimal state of consciousness. Top-level athletes are trained to get into, and stay in, their flow state for peak performance. Many of the biggest and most innovative companies understand the power of this. They see how this flow/receptive state can drive change and create new ideas and ways of working throughout their businesses. This is a very exciting concept for you on a personal level, whether you work for yourself, in a small business, or as part of a large corporation. Imagine what you or your team working in the state of flow could accomplish.

Everyone can move to a state of flow, simply by noticing your emotions.

Unsurprisingly, there have been many scientific studies about the receptive state. They have discovered that the body undergoes some incredible physiological and psychological changes when 'in flow'. Studies have shown that, when working, team members or top executives who were in their receptive state were five times more productive than those who were out of flow. You've probably noticed this; you get much more done when you're in a good mood, have clarity and focus. We'd all become more productive if we increased our flow state by just 20%. Using EAM, we'll show you how you can increase it a whole lot more.

Why Be in Flow?

There are many proven benefits to being in flow. Physically, it's shown to increase the fluid exchange into and out of cells, create better filtration of blood and fluids, and better absorption between the capillaries and tissues. These have long-term effects on health, too. Coherence (flow) creates measurable changes in hormonal activity and reduces adrenal and cortisol levels. All because you feel good! Ultimately, it creates a better efficiency of energy across the whole system.

On a psychological level, flow reduces the stress response while activating the relaxation response. This stimulates the production of brain chemicals that are associated with increased creativity, productivity and focus. There are marked changes in our ability to think clearly, recall and access information, as well as an increased emotional stability and sense of wellbeing.

Studies of people who use flow-building techniques have shown that being in a coherent state creates a measured drop in the effects of stress, increased positive mood and a change in the quality of life and attitudes. ALL from being able to manage our state of flow!

To fully understand how flow works in the body, let's take a look at research from the HeartMath Institute and Resonance Science Foundation. For more than 40 years, researchers here have studied the science behind electromagnetic energy, physiology and the way we experience the world. Much of their work is based on monitoring the electromagnetic influence of our heart and brain on the rest of our body and environment. They focus on a specific scientifically measurable physiological and energetic state called coherence – in other words, flow. Or, when out of flow (which we called resistance or reversal), they call incoherence. This has been shown to affect our thinking, emotions, perception and outlook on life. Their model is grounded in research into neurocardiology (the study of communication between heart and brain), psychophysiology (the study of physiological bases of psychological processes), and neuroscience (the study of neurons).

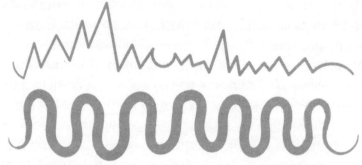

Representation of incoherent and coherent heart waves

In HeartMath, coherence is a specific measure of the heart's rhythms known as HRV (heart rate variability), which appears as smooth and orderly wavelike patterns. Incoherence is shown as a heart rhythm with erratic patterns. In coherence, all of our energy is flowing and there's a natural synchronicity in our body systems. During this time, many people experience more energy, feel more alive, are grounded or composed, and are able to think clearly. Physiologically, their body shows a more synchronized rate of breathing, better blood flow, improved nervous system function, boosted immune function and a better hormonal balance.

The HeartMath Institute has shown that everyone is capable of moving to this state of coherence, simply by noticing their current emotion and choosing to change it to something more positive – an emotion such as love, compassion or happiness. Within EAM, we use this same principle of choosing to shift emotions from an incoherent or resistant state to a coherent or receptive one. This process of recognizing our state and choosing to shift to a more positive one has been shown in studies to have multiple beneficial physiological and psychological impacts.

With EAM, the intention is to increase your capacity to successfully handle the energetic, mental and emotional responses to life, so you can create a greater sense of well-being, feel more connected and shift your internal baseline energy (set point) to a higher, more positive vibration.

Most people agree it's our *perception* of life, rather than the experience, that creates feelings of stress, anxiety and overwhelm. We know these are simply resistance. What if we could find a way to handle them better by changing our energy and the physiological effects they have on us? We can do this with EAM. We can choose to shift to a state of receptivity. If resistance is created through our perception, this changes our perception to a more positive one. To begin, we need a better understanding of what happens in our physiology, and the integral part played by our heart and brain in our cognitive, emotional and energetic experience of the world.

Research in the field of neurocardiology shows that the neurological connection between heart and brain is far more complicated than we ever thought; it really is fascinating. Studies have shown that information is consistently sent *from* the heart *to* the brain via our nervous system. Yes, you read that correctly. Our heart sends information to our brain as well as receiving information from it.

The Role of the Heart

Our heart is the most powerful electromagnetic communicator in the body. It can physically be measured up to 20 feet away on a machine called a superconducting quantum interference device (SQUID). Amazingly, the electrical measurement of our heart is up to 60 times greater in amplitude than our brain. And, energetically, what they're measuring is what we know as our aura (see p. 68).

Research has confirmed that our heart does much more than simply pump blood; in fact, it's a sensory organ that acts as a super-sophisticated information encoding and processing centre. This means that your heart is able to learn, remember and make *independent* functional decisions that *bypass* the brain. (Play some dramatic music, this is a big deal!) Our heart isn't only mechanical (pumping blood); it's also intelligent (processing and sending information). It's able to detect changes in our endocrine and nervous systems and influence them. Our heart creates its own hormones and neurotransmitters, a function previously believed to only happen in the brain, and these affect higher centres of the brain, which are involved in perception and emotional processing. Our heart is what keeps the rhythm and pace of the body. It is an amazing organ.

The maze of neural networks that connect the heart and cardiovascular system to the brain is far more extensive than those connected with any other major organ. This means more information is travelling **from the heart to the brain** than anywhere else in the body. WOW, WOW, WOW! This concept of energetic information being communicated through a neural network is actually seen in many biological systems. We see this in animals, trees, marine life. Now we can see that it also happens with human beings.

46

Some amazing studies have shown just what a coherent, receptive or in-flow heart can do. When meditating with a set intention to create a change, a person is able to use their heart coherence state to create physical, structural changes in water inside and outside of the body, the rate of growth in cells and structural changes in DNA. Cell growth can enhance by 20% with the energy of coherent intention, and the growth of tumour cells can be inhibited by 20%, too. This clearly shows that cells in your body respond to your flow state and intentions.

Let us clarify this. Your energy state, thoughts and emotions are measurably affecting your physical body. By using EAM, you can choose to change your frequency, set an intention and be able to change the structure of matter at a physical level. (Insert more dramatic music.) This again speaks back to the quantum physics experiment that proves we create our reality with our thoughts. As you'll see, it also ties beautifully into why we do Step 5 of EAM.

The Effects of Flow

On a physiological level, research shows that the flow state creates a neurological synchronization between the heart and brain. It changes structures and associations in our brains and changes brainwave patterns, which influence our body. It reduces adrenal and cortisol levels in the body, which resolves the physiological effects of stress that can create disease. Flow state promotes physical healing, as the body is able to return to normal function faster. It also releases tension in the body and muscles, relieves physical pain, reduces symptoms of illness and creates changes on a cellular level, too.

On a psychological level, research shows that habitual coherent states enable us to maintain positive emotions for longer. That means we can naturally and easily create more positive emotions. We also have better mental and emotional stability, and our ability to adapt to changes in our environment increases. By allowing yourself to be more receptive you actively seek more new experiences as your brain seeks to maintain the status quo of positivity in your environment. You're able to rewire the brain and create new emotional and mentally positive experiences.

The Effect of Being out of Flow

It stands to reason that the effects of incoherence (resistance or reversal) can affect us on a physiological and psychological level, too. This is more commonly known as stress.

We've all experienced stress in our lives. It is defined as 'the body's natural reaction to any change that requires an adjustment or response; these changes can be physical, mental and/or emotional'.

When stressed, our body is in the 'fight, flight, freeze and appease' response. You may have heard about this! It's the physiological response to an outside stimulus, and it has served us for a long time during evolution. It's designed as a short-term solution – to empower our body to run away from a big scary lion, or something life-threatening. Although there are fewer scary animals prowling the streets, the response is still useful as it gives us a short burst of energy, for the increased speed or strength in our physiology in anticipation of 'the attack'. It increases blood flow to muscles in the extremities, raises the heart rate, creates more tension in muscles and increases the blood-clotting functions in the body.

Stress engages and affects our entire body, including the nervous, respiratory, circulatory, immune, digestive and reproductive systems. These changes are designed to give the body the best chance of survival in the immediate moment. Essentially, stress shuts or slows down internal functions in our trunk. That energy, blood and oxygen are diverted to the muscles and bones on the arms and legs, so that they can do their best to protect us when under attack!

Again, this process is designed for a short-term benefit to the body to get out of immediate danger. It's no benefit to us in the long term. However, we live in a world that creates huge amounts of stress – real and perceived – with well-documented impacts on our body and energy systems. These include:

- A reduction of blood in our internal organs, meaning our body is more prone to attack from illness through bugs, bacteria and viruses. This is one of the main reasons so many people get sick under stress, or get extremely sick when a common flu, cold or virus is present. This is often less to do with the illness, and more with the internal environment. Our body is unable to deal with an externally perceived threat and an internal one at the same time.
- Affecting hormones and creating high levels of adrenaline and cortisol.
- Affecting normal physiological functions in digestion, heart rate, cell filtration rates and the growth and death phases of cells.
- The body being unable to heal itself and developing chronic physical health conditions, pain, inflammation and illnesses.
- Decreased brain function, creating negative associations in the brain. We're unable to think clearly, make logical decisions, or function at the highest levels.

- Being emotionally stressed, angry or irritable; getting stuck in negative emotions.
- Low mood, with little or no energy.

In comparison, when we're in flow, feeling love or in the growth phase, blood circulates to the central organs, heart, lungs, liver, digestive and reproductive systems. These are the essential organs in our body, which we need to be functioning effectively to maintain our health. When in flow, these organs work to maintain homeostasis.

Sadly, for many people stress is a normal part of everyday life. When it comes to changing your life, this understanding is vital. We have become so used to low-level resistance, we learn to cope until it's so dramatic it can no longer be ignored. Stress is so normal, for many people it's almost a badge of honour. How many times do you hear people say, *'I am SO stressed'* or *'I am SO busy'*!

Stress is far from 'normal'.

Pay attention to when you're feeling stress as it's a clear indicator that you may need to do EAM. Use the Five Steps to release any energy, thoughts and emotions you're feeling. Change your focus and align yourself to the most positive possible outcome for that situation. By doing this, you'll change neural pathways to create new associated patterns in the brain, which will influence your whole physical body, hormones and energy, too. Trust us … do it for yourself!

The Role of Emotions

Despite the common perception that thoughts trigger emotions, there's actually a more complex interplay of our energy, hormones, brain, nervous system, heart and body involved. Studies have shown that what helps create our emotional experience is the repeating and rhythmic patterns generated by our heart; whether they're in flow or out of flow, these patterns are like best friends to our brain. These heart wave patterns are compared to our energetic, emotional and mental 'set points'. Like default settings, our system will always revert to these baselines or standards, which are all tracked and managed via the brain stem. Signals are sent upward toward the thalamus, hypothalamus and amygdala – the parts of the brain centre involved in processing emotion. As well as sending information to the brain, our heart produces its own neurotransmitters (hormones) and sends signals throughout the body. These hormones also affect the brain and provide an important influence over our experience of emotion.

Knowing this turns previous understandings on their head (excuse the pun!). It's important to understand that our emotions aren't a cognitive or linear experience. Neuroscience has yet to determine the sequential process through which emotions happen. It's almost a simultaneous process. The actual experience of emotion is therefore made up of the heart, brain, limbic and processing systems, hormones, changes in electromagnetic energy sent from the heart, and a change from default set points. So, our emotional experience involves our whole body.

Molecules of Emotion

We have great respect for Candace Pert, an American neuroscientist. She sadly passed in 2013 and left an amazing body of work. Through her decades of research, Pert was able to show that our emotions aren't a figment of our imagination, they're real molecular structures located in our mind, body and energetically in our system. As we know, all matter has its own electron field, will be part of the unified field and is also connected to and interacting with your biofield, meaning the energy field or aura, which is inside and outside of your physical body. It is the field of energy that influences the inner and outer worlds. Her work has explained scientifically what many Eastern and ancient philosophies have known for centuries – consciousness comes before manifesting reality! We now know that in the physical body our emotions are little pieces of biochemical information created and sent as peptides (proteins) to their receptors, which are present on cells throughout our entire body. **This means our whole body system is geared to receive, read and store emotional information** (did we hear that music again?) and plays an integral part in our subconscious (or unconscious) memories, because emotional information is held within the body tissues.

In her book *Molecules of Emotion* (Simon & Schuster, 1999) Pert explains beautifully, 'it's becoming increasingly apparent that the role of peptides isn't limited to eliciting simple and singular actions from individual cells and organ systems. Rather, peptides serve to weave the body's organs and systems into a single web that reacts to both internal and external environmental changes with complex, subtly orchestrated responses. Peptides are the sheet music containing the notes, phrases and rhythms that allow the orchestra – your body – to play as an integrated entity. And the music that results is the tone or feeling that you experience subjectively as your emotions.'

Your Internal Reference

Our brain and body system is adaptive, always learning information and rewiring our neural networks according to the information we receive, and perceive, from our environment. The body will then maintain the environment according to what we know. We call the reference points naturally used by the body 'set points' – think of them as default settings. In the same way, our body maintains thoughts, beliefs, patterns, emotions, using our internal set points. Our brain is constantly reading information from environmental signals (meaning the energy field) to see how well something matches our internal set points or previous experiences. When these set points and our perception of the environment are a match to what we know or have previously experienced, we feel happy because we feel safe. When our thoughts, emotions, external inputs and energetic messages are a match to that feeling of safety, love or happiness, they're congruent so we feel great and release happy hormones like oxytocin and endorphins into our body.

This process applies to situations that may actually make you happy or sad. For example, you may be in a controlling relationship, which is hurting you emotionally. You're constantly upset, fearful and depressed. Even though you consciously know it's no good for you, you stay because it's what you know, therefore it feels 'safe'. To change this, we have to change our perception, neural networks and environment in order to create our new normal.

We experience a resistance or reversal when the messages our system is receiving from the environment create a mismatch to our internal baseline, putting us in a state of instability. This can be triggered by a thought, emotion or any other internal, external or energetic input, conscious or unconscious. In these situations, our normal experiences cannot easily be processed. Our neural system sees this as a mismatch to our past, present or future projections of experiences. It then sounds the alarm, which is what we experience as a negative feeling or emotion. This sends our body into that adrenaline-fuelled process because it perceives we are, or may be, in danger.

If we're unable to catch ourselves and pay attention to when we're out of flow, that instability is still there in our frequency. Have you ever noticed that bad days seem to spiral? You get up, you're in a bad mood, you stand on a plug, poor hot water out of the kettle on your hand, slam your fingers in a door and then the person treading on your foot gets it all offloaded on them. Instead of you saying, '*It's okay*', you're ready to start a fight! Your vibration is already on a high alert waiting for another situation to match its previous bad experience, which then creates more negative experiences.

It's also true of our good days getting better. Have you noticed that on those mornings when you jump out of bed feeling happy, something great happens? You tell your friends. Then you find money, get freebies and are told how much you're loved ... This occurs because we spend our time looking for positive happy situations or experiences that validate the patterns we're having, good or bad, positive or negative. The good news is that you can change your pattern with EAM!

This response also applies to the journey we're on now. As you start using EAM, it will feel like 'hard work' because you're doing something new. You may want to give up, and your mind will create a number of rational thoughts as to why that's a good idea. Knowing this, you can recognize the pattern, and once you know the Five Steps of EAM you'll be able to use them to move forward.

Our Brain and Nervous System

Neuroscientific developments allow us to see that there is more to our cognitive experience than the brain alone. Whereas we used to believe that our emotions originated in the brain, we now know that they're more an experience of the heart, brain and body all working together. Our brain works like an old-fashioned analogue processor that's constantly looking for patterns, similarities, differences and relationships between them. It's continuously trying to create a picture from the information it has.

The human brain weighs about 1.5 kg (3 lbs) and, energetically, runs on around 12 watts of power, which is a fifth of the power required by a standard 60-watt light bulb! It has 400 miles of capillaries and 86 billion microscopic neurons, which are in constant communication. To put that into context, they're making around 10 quadrillion calculations every second. And yes, that's a real number!

Each neuron in the brain is like a tiny tree connecting to other neurons, and where they touch one another they make between 4,000 to 9,000 connections. That's a lot of communication! It's almost too much to comprehend. These neural connections enable us to generate our experiences and perceptions in each moment. They guide us to think, create, understand, use reasoning and manage our emotions, memories and learning potential.

On a physical level, they're fundamentally tiny connections between different neurons in the body (as well as the brain).

You may have heard the term 'neurons that fire together wire together.' It was first used by the neuropsychologist Donald Hebb, known for his fabulous work in understanding the associative field of learning. In essence, what he means is that every experience we have – every thought, feeling and physical sensation – triggers thousands of neurons at the same time. These associations form a neural network – a simple pathway or groove in the road. And like any pathway, the more it's used, the stronger or deeper the connection becomes. As we repeat an experience over and over, the brain learns to trigger the same neurons each time.

This is a wonderful process and is what helps us learn, store and remember important information simply and efficiently. The good and bad news is that these neurons can be rewired to respond to a situation in a new way. This is great if we want to retrain our brain to have a more positive outlook. However when it's repeatedly used for unhelpful thoughts, habits or beliefs, or if we experience something traumatic, these can change our previously good experiences into ones that our brain says are to be avoided.

Our life experiences actually change the brain.

EAM teaches us a new process or way of being. By using EAM, we readapt and create new pathways in our brain; we literally rewire it. This process is called neuroplasticity – it's fascinating and it happens throughout our life. This is how we learn, create our experiences and connect information together on a neurological level. It was previously believed that our brain was fixed and immovable, and from a certain age it stayed the same. Research has now shown that our physical brain is evolving all the time. This process is our brain's capacity to create new connections between events and information; at the same time eliminating and cleaning old connections and strengthening the ones in use. Our brain is continually evolving and rewiring itself. How exciting is that?!

Do you remember all you learned as a baby? Nope, neither do we! You've forgotten because you no longer need this as an adult. This is a really important concept to understand, because previously we believed that the brain determines our life experiences. However, we've learned that **our life experiences and perceptions actually change the brain**. Please read that again. It's how *we* interpret information that influences the neural connections in our brain. As these new connections develop, we learn new habits, patterns and ways of being. This is powerful and one of the most exciting parts of what you can do when using EAM. By changing your perceptions of past experiences, and by creating positive new experiences, you're actually rewiring your brain! (Can we hear that orchestra again!)

Set Points

We've already discussed set points – our default patterns of being and behaving – when taking about our internal reference system (see p. 53), and we've seen how they can be either helpful or unhelpful depending on where your current set points are on a particular subject. We're creatures of habit, who want to feel safe. Our brain is always looking to create a match between our past and our new experiences. If it's unable to find a reference in our field or neurological programming, then it's outside of our comfort zone. As a result, we feel unsafe and can get 'stuck' in unhealthy set points. It's then almost impossible to create the lasting changes we want because our energetic and neurological patterns will bring us back to what the brain knows.

The only way to create change is to establish new set points by changing the connected information. That is exactly what we do with EAM. By creating new energetic and emotional experiences, the brain can associate this new information with that set point. This also enables us to rewire the brain and energy imprints in our aura. By changing our set points, we create a happy, healthy internal reference that provides safety and comfort. We will then seek out more positive life experiences to match our new status quo.

Energetically, on a universal level the set point is love. Our natural way of being is in flow = love, and we always want to get back to that receptive state. Anything outside of that creates resistant thoughts, feelings, patterns and emotions. This is all unconscious, yet it's what we're all searching for. Everything we do is about bringing us back to LOVE – the universal set point. It's this same process which keeps us pursuing happiness or love.

Focus and Attention

Have you noticed how sometimes a thought or belief can run away with you, and then sucks up your focus and energy on situations that are unhelpful? Yet, it's all energy that we've allowed to gather momentum and run away with us. If our brain is going through the process of sorting, distilling and generalizing information on our behalf, surely it's up to us to consciously allow ourselves to focus our attention on what *we* want, rather than what other people want us to believe, think or say.

Have you noticed how easily your mind can be side-tracked by social media, news, gossip or the media? We then lose half a day thinking, researching and talking about 1,001 situations that have nothing to do with our current experience, detract our energy or focus and send us off into a spiral of resistance! This is a habit we suggest you choose to break. It happens on mass consciousness level too – have you seen the domino effect of a few people in fear, which creates a stampede of unhelpful, reactive behaviour. This can lead to riots, and cause countries, economies and civilizations to crumble. Thankfully, you now have EAM to help you work on good daily habits.

Remember, we all have a choice about where we focus our attention. If we give it to situations that differ from where we are, or what we really want to do, we're creating our own resistance. It generates a pull between where we are now and where we really want to be.

Energetically, by giving your attention to a subject you flow energy toward it. The more energy you flow, the bigger it gets, the quicker it manifests. This works for the 'good' and the 'bad'. So, choose where you flow your focused attention energy. Remember the science in this. We create our reality. It's our observation that makes it exist in our life. If you no longer observe it, it will go. Choose to change the picture and focus, be receptive and in flow, giving energy to what you DO want instead. This is creating a new paradigm.

When focusing on our desire, we experience happiness because we're giving our thoughts, energy and emotions to that one thing, which moves us into the positive receptive state. We create a better connection and understanding of who we are, and feel safe, which supports us to achieve positive long-term outcomes.

We also solve problems more quickly when we're focused. We're more able to access the right ideas and thoughts. We get clearer pictures, ideas, inspiration and information because our energy is in the receptive state. By using EAM, you'll be able to keep your focus by maintaining your energy in the flow state. This process can also be instrumental in supporting you to change your life.

Positive Psychology

As a branch of science, positive psychology is less focused on what's 'wrong, sick, ill or weak' and is more focused on strength, ability and capability. The focus is on enabling people to find and build the best of themselves, to create the life they want.

Many self-help tools, psychology methods and counselling practices are focused on what's wrong – they are 'past-focused' as they seek to look for the root cause. No one is saying these are wrong, yet there is another way. EAM focuses on what's good, right and inspiring, and will take you where you want to go in life. The only time you 'look back' is to explore what's standing in the way of your alignment right now.

Many experts in the field of positive psychology define a few key elements that set it apart and these are also important within EAM. They include:

- Seeing the world through the lens of abundance, which enables you to expand and build on your own resources and to find answers and solutions. This mindset enables you to recognize that you have the capacity for everything.
- Believing that we all have the innate ability to grow, change and develop. Focusing on building our strengths and loving the good elements of ourselves.

- Focusing on our overall sense of happiness and wellbeing, which can be our level of life satisfaction, and positive emotions, and looking at fewer negative ones.
- The fact that we want to have a lasting sense of purpose and meaning, and experience self-development as a person. The purpose is to create more positive emotions, engagement in life, a greater sense of meaning, better relationships and a feeling of accomplishment.

These are key elements you need to be able to change your life. That is exactly what we want to share with you using the Five Steps of EAM.

In summary, we can see that our state of flow impacts every area of our life experience. Coming up, we'll explore more of the energetic, emotional and mental aspects of flow, and how you can use EAM to create and remain in the receptive state as and when you choose. Getting into, and staying, in this receptive state is about bringing your life together holistically, looking at your environment, your food, diet, relationships – well, everything! And, as you allow yourself to be more in flow, the quicker your life will change.

Chapter 4

YOUR ENERGY SYSTEM: GOING WITH THE FLOW

In this chapter, we'll explore our own energy systems and structures, to gain a deeper understanding of the power we hold within ourselves. By learning about the intricate correlations between ancient energy principles and modern science, we'll see how modern science is able to measure the effectiveness of such energy tools and techniques, helping to prove that working with energy does make a difference.

For this you may need to step outside of what you already know. Energy conforms to its own set of rules, which quantum physicists are still working to understand. If we organize, separate and squeeze it into a box, we lose the perspective that this understanding brings. Energy is multidimensional, all happening simultaneously, on all levels of the micro- and macrocosm, at all points in time. They're all connected.

We want you to recognize that you're a part of this field – you interact with it, create and define it in every moment. When using EAM in your life, you have an open doorway to consciously interact with it all.

Our Life Force

Now we're on the same page with energy, let's explore how this life force is interacting with us. The background to EAM is firmly grounded in Eastern philosophies. So let's begin the conversation there.

Qi

In Chinese medicine, all energy is referred to as Qi (or 'chi'). Qi means 'breath' or 'air', and describes the whole range of energy from non-physical into the physical forms. Qi always moves and is all-encompassing. It ascends and descends; it transforms and stores. Qi is also protective. It transforms food and air into Qi, which your body uses as fuel. Qi holds bodily functions in place; it creates form and structure, such as our bones and organs. It manages body size, weight, structure and shape. It keeps blood in the vessels and nourishes the organs. It warms and protects the body from illness, bacteria and viruses. Our aging process, physical health, mental and emotional wellbeing are all managed by Qi production and flow. You can see what's meant by everything is energy!

In the body, Qi acts more like a fluid, which has actually been found in the meridians. Modern understanding calls it bioplasma – this is the substance that operates at different frequencies to form our whole energy system: meridians, chakras, aura and each layer of our aura.

The overall purpose of EAM is to enable you to create a greater flow of Qi and be able to direct that flow in any way you choose. By doing this, you can influence every area of your experience – physical, mental and emotional – by deliberately directing energy to create changes in your health, environment, relationships, wealth and wellbeing.

The more energy work you do, the greater flow of Qi you allow in every area of your life, body and energy structures. The greater the flow of Qi, and the higher your vibrational frequency becomes, the better you're able to direct energy and attract what you want in your life.

Yin and Yang

In Chinese theory, the underlying principle is described as the 'Tao of one', meaning one source. This represents the foundation of life, which is one, and it becomes two, splitting into 'yin' and 'yang' elements. These terms are used to explain the relationship between two seemingly opposite phenomena. Yet, in truth, these two 'opposites' are connected and it's actually the movement from one to the other that creates the flow of life. For example, to describe the different times of day we'd call midday 'yang', and midnight 'yin'. They're opposite in nature – midday is bright and sunny and midnight is dark and moonlit. Yet, we cannot explain one without having reference to the other.

The yin–yang symbol

In general, the yin element is the more feminine element – dark, wet, soft, down and slow. Yang is the more masculine – light, dry, hard, up and fast. (You can draw any jokes you like from that!) Yin and yang define and describe the limitations of the experience we live within every day. The sun is unable to be higher than at midday. The sun is unable to be lower than at midnight. Nothing can be more feminine than a woman, and nothing more masculine than a man.

Everything in our lives has an element of yin and yang, including the journey to changing your life. In order to be high, you also experience the low. In order for it to be light, you also experience the dark. In order to experience happiness, you experience sadness. Without one you've no reference point, no context and no motivation to move to the other.

You can even see this in the flow of energy itself. Take a look at the carrier wave signal and notice its movement up and down. This is the movement between yin and yang, and all life goes through this process, including us.

Everything moves beteen yin and yang – that is true flow.

It's energetically impossible to be riding on a wave of high-vibrational flow all the time. It would be exhausting. So, please give up that myth. Rather than feeling downhearted, what this means is you're now free to truly get in flow. True flow means being able to ride the wave *between it all* – the ups and the downs – with as little resistance or push as possible. And this is exactly what you can do with EAM. Changing your life is about working with the flow between yin and yang, listening to inner guidance, knowing when to be active and when to be still, when to make progress and when to reassess. There is benefit in both, which is what *true flow* means. By using EAM you can work within this dynamic of yin and yang and learn to listen to your own vibration.

The same applies for people striving for 'balance' in their lives, between work and play. Look at the yin–yang symbol and you'll see that balance is an elusive concept that is incapable of existing. Balance is static, so would be represented by two semi-circles. Yin–yang shows movement, the constant flow between the two.

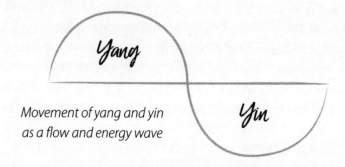

*Movement of yang and yin
as a flow and energy wave*

The Body's Energy Structures

Let's take a brief look at your energy systems and how they influence our daily life experience. If you remember from Chapter 1, all electromagnetic systems have a field. Our energy system is structured, and functions, in the same way. The electrical element that runs up and down is the power, like a battery. In the physical body, this flow of energy – head to toe – runs through funnels and key meridians. The magnetic part of our system, which attracts, draws and sends out signals horizontally, is mainly our heart and hara, and also the only horizontal meridian, Dai Mai. Our carrier wave element, which sends the messages into the wider world, comes from our vibrational heart energy, thoughts and emotions.

Your energy system begins its formation at conception. The outer layer of the egg is the outer layer of your aura. At the first split of cells (one becomes two), yin and yang meridians begin to flow and create forms and structures within the body. These also create two opposite, circular flows of energy, which move up the front (yin) and down the back (yang). These flows move into and outside the body. The first split also creates a channel through the middle of the body – in

Chinese medicine known as Chong Mai – and we refer to it as your funnel.

Picture a funnel shaped like a cone, coming down into your body (yang energy) meeting at your belly button and another coming out from the belly button (yin energy) into the earth. The funnel manages the quantity or strength of energy that flows throughout your energy system, and the bigger the better (never let anyone tell you otherwise!). Your funnel expands and contracts depending on your flow state. You can use EAM to deliberately adjust its size and, therefore, your capacity to consciously flow more potential energy. Imagine this is like your battery.

The second split of the egg creates your horizontal axis, which creates and manages your connections and interactions here on earth. When in the physical body, it flows through and around the hara. The meridian that manages this is known as Dai Mai and holds your energy field together. The other energy structures, channels, organs and associations develop during your time in the womb, after birth and at various stages in your life.

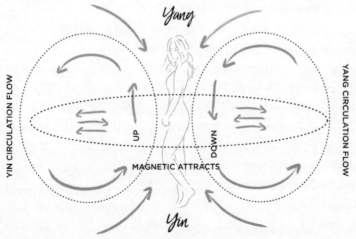

Energy flows show funnel flow, and yin and yang circulation of Qi

Your Aura

Our aura is our electromagnetic field generated primarily by our heart and influenced by our head and hara (see p. 81). We already know our heart energy can be measured up to 20 ft away from our physical bodies. Our aura enters a room before we do!

Your aura is made up of energetic layers, and your physical body is the slowest vibrating part of it. Have you ever experienced someone walking into the room behind you, and you can sense them without seeing or hearing them? Or have you met someone and had an instant like or dislike before you've even spoken to them? This is you reading the vibrations in their aura. If you could see it, your aura might look like a Russian nesting doll, with different layers, one outside the other, each one corresponding to various aspects of your life.

Your aura is a recording device – every thought, word, feeling, action and memory is held in the field.

Your aura is also a recording device. Every thought, word, feeling, action and memory (good or bad) has been stored in your energy field here, right from your time in the womb to now. We call them imprints, and these imprints create our resistances and reversals. Energetically, this is where we hold our conscious and subconscious information – like a logbook. Imagine your aura to be like an expanded 3D version of your experience, which you carry everywhere like a reference library. It's also a two-way communication system; it both transmits energy from us, based on what's in the library, into the outside world, and then receives and processes the information that comes back.

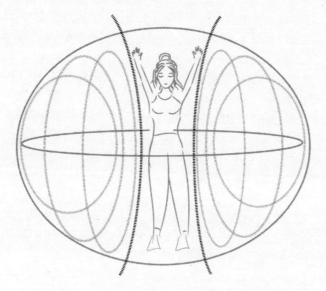

Your aura in flow, energy circulations with funnel

Our aura is the largest of our energy structures, containing everything within. It's forever changing: expanding or contracting, opening up, shutting down, depending on energy, thoughts, emotions, environment and our perception of life. Once you understand how your aura works, you can choose to deliberately work with it to change your life. Imagine we're cells of the wider planet – what you do to work on aligning yourself and create flow in your auric field will create a ripple out into your wider community

Everything we experience is an outcome of what we hold in this electromagnetic field; everything that's sent from and communicated to us is filtered through what exists in the different layers of our aura. This means that our previous experiences held in our energy influence every moment, even when we're no longer in that situation.

With this understanding, you'll see that what's already in your aura defines your experience. What you perceive in life is filtered through your aura layers, which we know are imprinted with past experiences. So, you'll judge what you see or hear through your own filter. This is why two people can be in a situation and see or hear exactly the same thing, yet interpret it differently.

This means that the thoughts, beliefs, emotions and experiences you hold in your energy field will continue to reflect and repeat in your life until you shift them. Seriously, underline that bit. It may be one of the most important sentences in the book. Now that you know this one thing, you have the potential to change your life because you can change your energy with EAM. This is exactly what EAM is designed to do.

How Our Aura Is Structured

Each layer of our aura vibrates at a particular energy frequency. The further away from the physical body, the higher the vibration. When you are in flow, each layer of your auric field is like a big, strong connected mesh network, like a beautiful spider web. This web can become broken, with holes, gaps, cracks, dents or fissures based on what happens in your energy.

The first four levels are our earthly energy bodies – physical, etheric, emotional and mental – and they interact with us on a day-by-day basis. We experience them all the time. This is the part of us that shapes who 'we' define as us, the individual. Outside of them, we have different energy levels that relate to our past lives (for those of you who believe in past lives), karma, our spirit lives and our connection to the rest of the planet, the rest of the electron field and the universe.

Physical Body
This part of our aura we can see, feel and experience easily. It's what we perceive as who we are. It's made up of our physical body, bones, organs, blood, nervous system, tissues and cells. It is the slowest vibrating part of our energy field. The healthier your physical body is, the quicker and easier you manifest. When we meditate, our consciousness leaves the physical layer of our aura as we travel off to explore higher frequencies.

Etheric Body
Our etheric body is the next layer out and is usually found 0–12 inches away from the body. It's a representation of what's happening energetically with your physical body. You'll feel resistance here first, which is what we experience as symptoms before they become chronic physical conditions. This layer is the last warning system of the impact of imprints in other layers before it becomes physical.

Emotional Body
The next layer out is emotion, found 12–18 inches away from the body. It holds imprints of past emotional experiences, shocks and traumas. What we feel as fear and powerlessness is this layer shrinking in or collapsing down. Conversely, what's felt as love or happiness is this layer expanding.

Mental Body
The mental layer is found 18–24 inches away and is where we hold our beliefs, thoughts, patterns and memories. This layer is very much connected to the conscious (and unconscious)

mind. It's absorbing information all the time. It evolves as we grow, keeping a record of all past experiences.

In addition to these first four layers of our aura, there are three outer layers, which are known as heavenly energy layers and represent the more spiritual aspects of our lives.

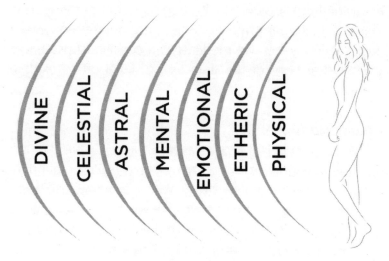

The seven earthly layers of your aura

Astral Body
Our lower and upper astral levels contain what are known as our 'Akashic records' – life lessons or 'karma'. The lower astral contains the messages of things that are actively being played out or need to be learned in this life, and our upper astral is the record of those previous and future life experiences.

Celestial Body
The celestial level is said to be where your spirit guides are. If you believe in angels, gods, other ascended masters and

teachers or other non-physical beings, they vibrate at this frequency. This is often why people need to meditate and get themselves into a vibrationally receptive state in order to hear their messages. The more in alignment you are, the more easily you hear and receive these messages.

Divine Body

The divine level is about our connection to everything else – mass consciousness, the planet and the wider universe. In science, this is where we merge with the unified field; where we all reconnect as one.

As you begin your EAM journey, focus on working on your earthly bodies in your aura. As you do, the others will naturally start to come into play. What's wonderful is that everything is imprinted in your aura. Using EAM, you'll be able to identify what's in your way, release it and align to something more positive to get back in flow.

Your Meridians

Each layer of your aura also has a set of meridians. These have been known to Chinese medicine for thousands of years. Scientists recently confirmed the existence of meridians (Jing Mai) as an integral part of the cardiovascular system. They found that tubular structures containing fluid (bioplasma) exist inside and outside of blood vessels and lymphatic vessels, as well as on the surface of internal organs and under the skin. Meridians are inside and outside of the body; they loop out of our fingers and toes and back into the body. Imagine tendrils of energy, reaching out and reading information in our aura. There are eight channels known as 'extraordinary meridians', which operate differently and are more like seas of energy we can tap into and direct. These hold the form and function of our whole energy system.

Representation of the main meridian channels (Jing Mai) through the body

You may have already heard about meridians. They're the energy equivalent of veins and arteries. The major meridians allow Qi to travel up and down our entire body system, connecting major organs. They're supported by smaller meridians named nadis, which act like capillaries moving Qi into the finer tissues and networks. Picture these like the structure of a leaf. There are various points where they come to the surface of the body and the energy can be directly accessed. Many therapies work on meridians including acupuncture, acupressure, massage, reflexology, kinesiology and EFT tapping.

In Chinese philosophy, your meridians are like energetic receivers of information. They contain different types of Qi as well as controlling the flow of blood and fluid. Their channels flow yin and yang energy from heaven and earth through the body. It's this flow of Qi through us that creates our health and illness. Each meridian acts as a direct channel for the associated organs within the physical body as well as representing different mental, emotional, psychological and physiological elements in the body. It's these meridians that allow communication between our external world and our internal organs. In addition to our chakras (see below), our meridians also enable the energetic communication of information from our aura into our physical body.

Your Chakras

Chakra is a Sanskrit word meaning 'wheel'. It's used to describe any number of energy centres in our physical and energetic bodies. While they are part of Ayurvedic medicine, rather than Chinese medicinal philosophy, traditionally they're prominent in practices based in Hinduism and Buddhism, such as yoga, mantras and meditation. It's important to include them in this book because they have meaning in the work we do with EAM and help provide a complete picture of your energy system. Chakras are energetic points that connect to our physical and energetic bodies, so they can commune with one another. There are believed to be 88,000 chakras within our body (major, minor, mini and sub chakras). They help maintain our aura's physical structure, and act as a powerhouse as well as a communication system. Most people know about the seven main chakras and these are the ones we will talk about here.

Chakras form part of the core of who we are. They correlate to the different levels of our aura and aspects of our physical, emotional and mental wellbeing. As we grow, our life experiences are also stored here as well as in our aura. As we create imprints, resistances or reversals, they affect the chakras and all associated connections at that developmental stage.

Again, until we resolve them vibrationally, we'll see these issues reflected throughout our lives.

Each chakra spins in a clockwise or counter-clockwise direction, acting like pumps or valves for the aura layers. Each chakra in our physical body interacts with the body via the associated endocrine gland and its group of nerves called a plexus. This is how each chakra can be linked with particular parts of the body. In the same way that your nerves read temperature or feel sound vibration, they also read your energy field. It's through the nerve plexus that imprints from your auric layers are communicated into your physical body and associated organs. This is one way that our thoughts and emotions in the energy field become physical symptoms and health conditions.

When we're in a receptive state, our chakras are open, more energy is cycled to the relevant layer of our aura, and we expand. The more shut down or smaller the chakra, the more the correlating aura layer will also shrink. This is due to resistances or reversals from imprints in our energy. Our chakras can be open, closed, implode, congested, deficient, get stuck and shatter. This is one way that we experience feelings, sensations or emotions in our energy.

How Our Chakras Are Structured

Our chakras have a powerful energy, which projects out from the front and back of the body. We have a set of chakras on each level of our aura, which help to maintain the flow of Qi and communication across the layers. For example, you have a sacral chakra on each level of your aura. Because they're all interconnected, when you release resistance at one level you also release this on other levels of the energy body where any resistance or reversals have occurred. The seven main chakras follow the structure of our spine.

The seven main chakra locations

The Crown Chakra (Seventh Chakra)

This represents our connection to our higher selves, higher consciousness, and connection to our divine energy levels.

The Third Eye (Sixth Chakra)

This is connected to our ability to be clairvoyant, our sensitivities to energy, and our intellect and perception of life. It represents our ability to connect to vision or intuition, and foresight into the future. As your third eye opens it enables you to see greater possibilities for yourself and others.

The Throat Chakra (Fifth Chakra)

This represents our ability to speak and clearly communicate our heart's truth. Speaking our truth from a place of love is like bathing the world in a healing vibration.

The Heart Chakra (Fourth Chakra)

Described as the bridge between the higher energy centres and our connection to our earthlier chakras. It's where yin and yang meet and where your soul is located in its physical form. Our heart energy is distinctly connected to our emotions. Our heart represents love for ourselves and others; it is our heart that enables us to connect and which governs our relationships. This chakra is all about unconditional love.

The Solar Plexus (Third Chakra)

Known to be a powerhouse that represents our self-esteem, willpower and personal responsibility here on earth. It's one of the three earthly chakras. Very often, this chakra is associated with our mental energy, beliefs and thoughts. It enables us to centralize and radiate light like the sun.

The Sacral Chakra (Second Chakra)

This is often associated with healing, creating and sexual energies. It's a generating life force and the basis of our physical vitality. The expression is pure power in taking the right action and it's like warrior power: strong yet humble, and flexible in our energy.

The Base Chakra (First Chakra)

We develop this chakra first and it provides the foundation on which we build the rest of our life. It's our connection to safety, security and stability. This chakra represents the most material aspects of ourselves. It's connected to sexuality, self-identity and our purely physical bodies. This chakra grounds our energy to the earth.

How Our Energy Creates Our Experience

Now you have a better understanding of the body's main structures: your aura, funnels, chakras and meridians. It's an integrated, multi-levelled system working simultaneously in harmony.

Our energy systems create and receive our experience.

Every time we think a thought, experience an emotion, have a conversation or see something in our environment, there's an associated reaction in our energy system. This reaction creates a non-linear sequence of events, which may open and close chakras, stop or flow Qi through our meridians and organs, expand or contract aura layers. At the same time, we're also experiencing the thought, emotion or conversation a particular way BECAUSE of what's already in our auric field. We're both creators and receivers of our energetic experience.

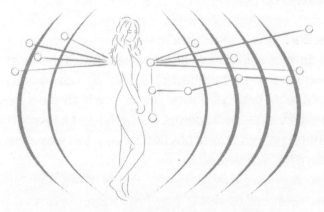

An energetic reaction in the energy field – 3D firework

If we could see this in our field, it looks like a 3D firework explosion in your aura, as your subconscious reactivates all of the information regarding that subject at once. Imagine lines connecting balls in different layers of your aura. For example, when you think about a person you've had a big argument with, an explosion will open up – it's connecting a ball of thoughts and memories on a mental level, another ball on the emotional level, along with a connection in the astral level where you were together in a past life. It shuts down your heart chakra as you palpitate, your sacral and base chakras shrink, you get *that* feeling inside and your legs go wobbly.

Resistance in the Energy Field

If you could see what's happening in your energy field, you would notice the resistances and reversal like 3D objects. Imagine it's filled with balls, blobs, lumps, bumps, cords, attachments, drains, leaks, cracks, fissures. Some would be the size of a grain of sand, some the size of a house! All of them have different vibrational densities. When we come to using the Five Steps of EAM, the wording in the Step 4 statement, '*I release this in all forms*,' refers to getting rid of these resistances.

We've all experienced the effect of resistances, all the time, maybe never knowing what they were. For example, that feeling in your heart when you think of someone who hurt you. Or that pain in your shoulder when you remember the 'friend' who talked behind your back. You'll use this concept a lot in EAM with Step 3, when we come to describe what is happening in your energy. It's useful to know that if you imagine you have a red, hard blob in your foot when you think about a certain person, you probably do!

You now have a much clearer picture of the different struc-tures that make up our energy fields, how they're connected and shape your experience. With this understanding can you see how important it is to clear up your vibration if you want to change your life? By using EAM to release resistance or reversals you can move from a feeling of being stuck to one of free-flowing Qi.

There's no need for you to understand any of these correlations in detail for EAM to work. However, they may help you uncover new places to explore, or understand why energy is moving through your body in a particular way, and why energy may express in particular locations. All of these will empower you when you start using the Five Steps of EAM.

The Three Energy Centres

In EAM, we have simplified all of these incredible, complex and multi-levelled experiences in the body into three main energy centres. These blend the neuroscientific and Eastern philosophical understanding of our energy. Two of these centres are your **head** and your **heart**, the third is your **hara** – a creative energy centre. Think of these as energetic concepts and functions rather than physical structures. These centres also work in a multidimensional way.

These are three fundamental and powerful electro-magnetic communicators, and we often use them in everyday language. We say, '*I am stuck in my head*', or '*I follow my heart*', or '*It's my gut feeling*' if something feels 'right' deep inside you. It's useful to understand the functions these energy centres have in our lives.

Our head energy is used to describe our mental and psychological lives, or any kind of brain activity. As an energy, it's more than just the physical brain structure, it also refers to consciousness and subconsciousness in our energy field. When we talk about the heart, we're referring to anything that is emotional and intuitive. The heart is where 'we', our unique point of consciousness, lives. With our hara energy, we're referring to the processes of assimilation, sorting, action, creation, manifesting into physical and our primal sexual power, force and drive.

EAM energy centres – your head, heart and hara

It's the alignment and function of these energy structures that creates and shapes our whole life experience. They're guiding us *all the time* yet are very often ignored. We're taught to use 'logic' or 'brain power' when our heart already knows the answer. Then, when situations go wrong we feel unhappy because we knew inside we could have chosen to listen to ourselves. Ever had that experience?

Imagine these three energy centres are like the energetic power behind a broadcasting tower. They are all sending and receiving messages, but when they become disconnected or out of sync, the messages are unable to be seen, felt or actioned. We can become so accustomed to this that we spend years living with them out of alignment, never realizing our energy system has been giving us the answers all along.

In EAM, we use the term 'alignment' to mean that these three energy centres are sending a congruent message. When we experience misalignment (feeling out of flow), it's because there's a 'disagreement' between them.

When we experience resistance, it's because these three centres are out of sync or sending mixed messages. For example, your head is *thinking* one thing and your heart is *feeling* another. Or you've made a decision with your head that you know is right in your heart yet you've stopped taking action with your hara.

When we experience something positive, we call this state 'energy alignment'. This means the centres are in sync and sending congruent messages. Magic happens – when these are working together, everything will manifest more easily into your life.

They're also a pathway for manifestation. Imagine a thought or idea coming in like a parcel above your head. We need the vision, planning, decision-making energy of the head; the peace, coherence, emotions, leadership and knowing from the heart; and the powerful action-taking, creating, manifesting energy of our hara to bring it into our physical everyday experience. To make it solid and real. This is one pathway of the process of manifestation.

If you're talking, thinking, feeling and taking action in your life with hate, fear, anger, guilt, blame, this will be sent out and will be what you attract back. Conversely, when doing this with love, happiness, gratitude, this is the message that's sent, so it's what you'll receive. Let's see how each of these powerful structures are made.

Our Head

Energetically, our head energy is made up of the higher chakras above the heart – the crown, third eye and elements of throat chakra. It encompasses what you'd consider to be 'logical' thinking, and controls our beliefs, patterns, memories, traits and thoughts.

The brain controls our nerves and hormones, and makes decisions. It controls elements of our psychology and our physiology and sends messages all over the body. When you're in hospital, what are the two organs they measure when on life support? They measure the electromagnetic activity of brainwaves and heart waves, and if either one fails to work you're considered to be dead. However, your head energy does much more than keep you alive. It travels way beyond the reach of our skull where, energetically, our thoughts project and connect to mass consciousness, and we also receive information, guidance and 'downloads' through here too.

Your head function is so important – think about its location on the top of the body. It's a 'lookout': it enables us to 'see' what's happening around us, to 'listen' to what's going on. It enables us to read the electromagnetic and vibrational energy and decipher it into something meaningful. It's the antenna that receives energetic information, thoughts and ideas.

Your head is an important and powerful source for defining experience. It filters information based on previous experiences and information we already hold. If we're inexperienced with life, never being exposed to new ideas, thoughts and concepts, we're limited. This will persist unless we receive new information to process and access. By opening up our head energy, we can increase our capacity to think clearly and receive new insights.

Your head energy has two functions: to send or receive, then to process information. Here's what happens in the three energy states.

Reversal

You're unable to send out clear messages, get clarity or make choices about what you really want. Your brain will re-fire neurological set points made at the time of the reversal, unable to be positive. In extreme cases, you may have mental disturbances and flashbacks.

Resistance

Conflict in your energy will result in chaotic thinking with less activity in the frontal cortex. You'll have resistant thoughts and beliefs, which hold you back.

Receptive

When in flow, it's our head energy that defines the new clear thought, belief or message. When receiving, this energy makes 'sense' and assimilates information into something cognitive, logical or sensible. Your brain and chemistry will create oxytocin and serotonin in the body. You'll have an active frontal cortex, clear thinking and brain function, greater insights, clarity of vision and more 'aha' moments, when everything comes together and makes sense.

You can see how important our head energy is. Let's see how it connects to our heart and hara.

Our Heart

Think about its location in the centre of our body – functionally everything has to go through the heart centre to communicate with each other. It governs our connection to others. Housed in the most protected parts of our body, behind the ribs, this is where our soul consciousness lives. In Chinese medicine, it's known as the emperor, held safe inside the walls of the temple. In acupuncture, to reset the whole body we need only treat the heart. Everything else falls into place. Energetically, it includes elements of the throat, heart, thymus and solar plexus chakras.

Our physical heart is responsible for the free flow of blood and oxygen around the body. It's our heart that feeds our head. We already know how magical our heart can be. Traditionally, we've been taught to believe that our head rules our heart. It's almost ingrained in us; people say, *'Don't follow your heart, you need to think that through.'*

However, remember our heart is clever – it's also controlling our nerves, hormones, physiology and pathology (see p. 46). Think about this. There have been many tragic cases of people who are clinically 'brain dead', yet their hearts are still pumping blood around the body. This makes a powerful case for the intelligence and autonomy of our heart, the fact it may be doing more than being a mechanical pump.

Here's what happens to it in the three energy states.

Reversal
Your energy is shut down. Your aura will be small. Heart rate variability (HRV) will be incoherent. Physically, long-term stress, adrenal exhaustion, chronic heart and lung health conditions, and issues with circulation can occur.

Emotionally, there is overwhelming fear, depression and a feeling of trapped, repeating emotions. There can be PTSD-type symptoms, mental health issues and feeling 'detached', disconnected or shut down from life and reality. While these may sound like head energy disturbances, in energy medicine these are all considered to be a disturbance of the heart. In

Chapter 6, we'll show you how you can create more alignment and open up your heart.

Resistance
Your energy bodies would be contracted, emitting resistant vibrations, incoherent heart patterns, elevated heart rate, stress, anger, frustration, jealousy and rage. Life will feel chaotic and out of sync. I am pretty sure that we've all experienced this at one time or another!

Receptive
All of the benefits of flow state can be attributed to the heart. The even rhythm of energy between the yin and yang, the free flow of Qi, blood and fluid in all energy systems, and coherent function. You feel contentment, happiness, empowerment, peace, joy, love and freedom.

Our Hara

Our hara energy centre can be located two thumb widths below your belly button. It's often called the lower *Dan Tien*, and contains elements of solar plexus, sacral, base and earth chakras. While the core of your hara is located there, energetically the hara refers to creativity, your ability to receive, your capacity to manifest and your sexual energy. Physically, it manages the actions of everything from your waist, below your belly button and into your groin and legs.

Unlike the head (brain) and heart, there is no physical organ for the hara. Its role is to create and manifest into the reality and govern our horizontal experience – our interactions with the world around us: things we can reach out and touch. It manages the key earthly elements of our life experience and is about grounding, strength and power.

This is the most mystical centre, in that it has the power to create matter from nothing or potential energy, to bring it into reality. Two haras – yin (the woman) and yang (the man) – come together to create life itself. Containing information passed down through the generations, it's the source of life force energy, and governs our physical development. Our hara energy is powerful – it's the foundational, grounding energy that enables us to be alive.

Now, if our body has the power and knowledge to build, create and grow a tiny, perfect human being, do you think it could also manifest what you want in life, too? Your ability to create or manifest is directly related to the flow of your hara. If you think of common terms, such as the Law of Attraction, it's the magnetizing, attractive, power force of your hara that allows you to manifest.

So, if you're having issues in manifesting, feeling abundant, creating or holding onto money, wealth or happy relationships, your hara is the place to look. It's one of the most powerful places to begin when using EAM. As you increase the receptivity in this energy centre, you'll watch your life transform. We love the hara!

Let's take a look at what happens to it in the three energy states.

Reversal
When your hara is in reversal, you feel disconnected from life, have no drive, are always exhausted and everything's a struggle. There might be chronic health issues with the womb, vagina, penis, prostate, bowels, kidneys, bladder, legs and anything from the belly button down. It's also associated with signs of dementia, issues with memory loss, depression and anxiety, and physical growth, development and learning difficulties. You may be withdrawn and unable to connect

sexually with yourself or partner, or battling with family or hereditary patterns on an energetic, mental, emotional or physical level.

Resistance

You disconnect from your inner power. Life feels 'hard'. It's difficult to manifest and instead feels like more 'work'. There might be acute health issues with the womb, vagina, penis, prostate, bowels, kidneys, bladder, legs and anything from the belly button down. Your level of arousal would be low and you'd feel exhausted no matter what you eat or how much you sleep.

You may notice this especially after childbirth, when the hara being opened can significantly deplete your whole energy. This may be one of the biggest reasons so many mothers change emotionally after birth. They aren't aware of the energetic impact of giving birth (especially if they've had a caesarean section or difficult labour and delivery). You could be withdrawn from people, especially partners or lovers. You may make love with hesitancy or because you feel you should, yet remain distanced from the act.

Receptive

Here, you are able to manifest and create magic. What you think, feel or ask for will manifest at amazing speed, driven and motivated by a force deep inside you. Your body will produce oxytocin and serotonin. For women, you'll experience powerful full-body orgasms and create a strong pelvic floor. Men will have increased strength and stamina when making love and be able to withhold ejaculation. Emotionally, you experience love, feel in a state of arousal and are attracted to the people and world around you. You're also 'attractive' to others and they're drawn to you.

The Power of Our Sexual Energy

While we're discussing the hara, we have to talk about sex. This topic – a whole book in itself – is often the root of most of our issues in life. For many reasons, we've disconnected from our hara and therefore our creativity, our ability to manifest and our sexual power.

Sexual energy is one of the most powerful, attractive manifesting forces there is. We know this – when someone is good looking or appealing, we say they're 'attractive' or have a 'magnetism'. You know, those people who oooooooze energy when they walk in a room. People can feel the attractive power from our hara, and we want your hara to be so open and powerful that it bowls people over when you walk into the room. Even if you're wearing your most unattractive pyjamas. Your hara is about much more than sex.

Yet, it's also the most misused of energies. Sexual energy is often used to control, or take power over others, or we shut it down to protect ourselves. It can also be depleted through over-activity, whether through too much sex or masturbation.

Our most in-flow moments are when we orgasm. Why? Because we've let go of our resistance and go with the moment. All of your energy centres – head, heart and hara – are in alignment, sending a congruent message. Have you noticed that when you're stressed, tired, overwhelmed or overthinking, it's almost impossible to reach climax? Because your vibration is in resistance, or maybe even reversal, and your energy centres may be shut down. For some, sex is something they have disconnected from. Emotionally, they are unengaged or detached, which means they've also lost connection to their most potent energy and the ability to use it to manifest or attract into every area of their life.

If we have experienced trauma, our brain (head) can literally disengage from seeing any sexual clues. This closes off the entry to yang energy into your funnel, so there is no flow of arousal energy coming down the funnel to the hara and genitals. This happens for both sexes, although more easily seen in men, who may be aroused one minute then lose the feeling the next, simply with a thought. Likewise, if we're in our head, thinking about our to-do list, it will reduce flow through our hara, and we're unable to experience ecstasy. Similarly, if we're hurt and disconnected from our heart, this changes how we communicate with others and affects our sexual and creative life force.

This also means that our unhealed reversals and resistance – in the form of imprints, thoughts, beliefs and experiences, sexual or otherwise – impact the flow of energy. These can come from anywhere, although are often found in the hara, where they hinder the flow that creates desire, arousal and orgasm.

If any of this resonates with you, this will be a great place to begin to explore and open up your hara with EAM, in order to change your life. We want you to be in your creative sexual power, more in alignment, with greater ability and speed to change your life.

You now have an understanding of these three key energy centres. When they're all in alignment, your structure is strong, you'll send congruent messages and manifest with ease, and life will feel awesome. Your yin and yang energy can flow and you're fully supported to start expanding yourself in all directions in your life. In Part Two, we'll introduce you to EAM and the sway, a powerful technique that will show you how to bring these energy centres perfectly into alignment.

Our Energetic Influence

So far, we've discussed Qi and the fact that everything is energy. We've explored how our energetic bodies are structured and contribute to our life. Before we move on, there are some other powerful aspects of your energy that are key to your understanding when manifesting and using EAM.

The Power of Visualization

Your mind is powerful. How you create your reality is through the power of your thoughts and perception of life. Your mind has no idea how to decipher the difference between what's 'real' or imagined, so there's power in visualizing – yourself, your life and future, or any situation – to create the best outcome. Your subconscious will then go about finding situations and scenarios that are a match to what you've imagined. We will explore this more in Chapter 6.

Your Energy

Remember, everything is energy. In simple physics, electrons of a like vibration will gather together through their magnetism. Think of the formation of a planet, drawing rocks into its gravitational field. The more that gather, the bigger it gets, the more physical it becomes. It gains momentum, attractive force and pace.

When it comes to your energy flow, be conscious where you direct it, what you give your time, energy and attention to. The more attention you give to any subject, the more momentum it gathers, the more manifested it becomes. These rules apply to all of us for everything, the good and the bad.

Your role is to notice how you feel in every moment. What is the 'quality' of your energy? If something feels 'off', apply EAM so it disappears before it grows. If something feels amazing, amplify that, feel into and expand it with Step 5.

Become conscious of your energy – do you feel tired or awake? What happens with certain foods you eat, water you drink, people in your space, activities you take part in, how much sleep you get? These are all indications of your energy – it all matters and you're receiving these signals about your energy state all the time.

Your Thoughts

Our thoughts are powerful waves of energy (remember our head is one of our electromagnetic communicators). You may have heard, *'Your thoughts create your reality'*, or *'You get what you think about'*, or *'You become the thoughts you think the most'*. All of these statements are true (when tied up with the emotions that match them, we'll talk about that in a minute).

Whether you're thinking positive thoughts or resistant thoughts, the same laws of momentum apply. If you want to perpetuate the story of your life as it is now, keep doing, thinking and saying the same as you do already. Nothing will change. Momentum and the Law of Attraction will bring those same vibrations and situations back to you.

Likewise, if you're ready to change your life, you have to recognize thoughts that are getting carried away in the wrong direction. Every time you think, a wave of energy is sent, which resonates throughout your auric field and is stored in the mental layer; do they all serve you? While science can only measure our brain waves at a short distance, many studies show that thoughts can travel long distances and affect cells, people or situations in that location.

Once our thoughts pass the boundary of our aura, they become part of mass consciousness. In the same way, we read mass consciousness, whether it's a group of people in a room, town or country, or perhaps some strange phenomena that grips the whole planet. In nature, it's the same process that creates a stampede when there is a lion, or that allows thousands of people at a concert to feel connected and united as one. You're tapping into that energy of mass consciousness every day. By consciously transforming our own thoughts to reach a higher vibration, and deliberately sending that out, we're changing mass consciousness and changing the world.

Our three flows of energy also apply to our thoughts. A reversed thought is known as a limiting belief; a resistant thought is known as a negative belief and a receptive thought is known as a positive belief.

Three Flows of Thoughts

Reversal	**Resistance**	**Receptive**
Limiting Belief	Negative Belief	Positive Belief

EAM – three flows of energy in thought form

With EAM, you can change thoughts that are unhelpful and imprint or create new ones. This means you change your reality! Deep, right? Your thoughts are part of your energy. They influence your life experience and the wider world, so become aware of them.

Your Emotions

We've already talked a little about emotions. Physiologically, they're created by our heart, brain, hormones and nervous system. Your emotions are also powerful waves of energy and are stored in the emotional layer of your aura.

Our emotional experience has a lasting impact on life – we remember more about how we *felt* in a situation than what we said or thought at the time. Your emotions are your main guidance system, there to give you clear indication of your current vibration. It's really simple: low mood = low vibe; good mood = high vibe.

These wavelengths influence your physical body and health; your cells are listening to how you feel and your vitality will respond accordingly. Like thoughts, your emotions send information out into your immediate environment (which, by the way, other people can read – we're no good at hiding

Three Flows of Emotions

←	←→	→
Reversal	**Resistance**	**Receptive**
Fear	All Other Emotions	Love

EAM – three flows of energy as emotions

our mood!). They also contribute to the mass or group consciousness.

When you think about the three flows of energy on an emotional level, true fear is a reversed emotion, and all other emotions are various degrees of resistance, with love being the most receptive or in flow.

The quickest and easiest way to start consciously working with your flow state is to pay attention to how you feel, to your emotions and physiological experiences. Once you understand EAM, you'll be able to use it to shift the resistant or reversed emotions, and change emotional set points in the brain and in your frequency. We can then create new associations in the brain and in our energy to create a better emotion or experience.

Within EAM we've developed our own energetic model of emotions, based on Dr David Hawkins' vibrational scale of consciousness.

At the bottom of the emotional scale is fear, the lowest vibrational emotion. True fear is debilitating. Energetically, it freezes our energy – imagine a deer in the headlights – it stops us in our tracks. In EAM terms, this would be a true reversal, which closes down our energy centres and chakras, shrinks the aura and makes you contract and be small.

At the highest point on the scale is the emotion of love. This opens and expands our life force – love is growth, connection. It's what happens when you love someone; you throw open your arms, you receive, you connect, you do and think good things. Love is the most receptive state you can be in. It's true flow. All other emotions are somewhere on the vibrational frequency between these two – fear and love – and represent resistances in varying degrees. It's impossible to feel fear and love at the same time, even though you can have multiple emotions on the same subject and different aspects of the situation.

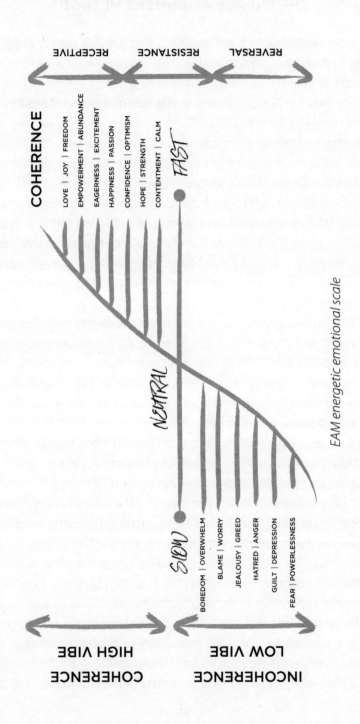

EAM energetic emotional scale

Your emotions all have meaning, and each of our emotions has its own energetic vibration – its own frequency – sent out from our energy.

For every emotion, there's a **vibration** and an **intensity** – and they are different. Our vibration is like the quality of the emotion; some are a low vibration, such as feelings of fear and depression; some are high vibrations, such as love, freedom and abundance. With the intensity, you can see the strength of the emotion measured by its distance from the neutral line. The further away the more power and strength it has, toward the middle you see there's less energy and therefore less intensity. This relates to their 'manifesting' power in your life. The greater the strength of emotion, the quicker the manifestation.

The emotional scale goes from contracted feelings on the left to feelings of expansion over on the right. In order to manifest, or live a life of happiness, we want to live our lives above this point of neutral – which means we're spending time in feelings of calm, contentment, happiness, passion, love and joy. These emotions tell you that you're in alignment. The closer to the neutral line means there may still be some resistance in comparison to the emotions of love.

We can have resistance to experiencing positive emotions like love or happiness. Remember as a child, how many times were you told to sit down or be quiet when you were happy or having fun? This can create resistance to feeling happy!

If you're spending time feeling irritation and frustration, how can you manifest the life you want? Have you noticed those people who seem to move from one drama to another? This is usually because they're vibrating emotions of fear, anger or feeling overwhelmed. They're probably talking to their friends, family and anyone who'll listen about why life is unfair, what is going wrong or what someone has done to them. All it would take is a simple shift of their frequency to stop the drama, yet most people are unaware that's all they need to do.

You'll use this emotional scale a lot to work with EAM. How many times do you think you've experienced fear? Or jealousy? How many of these feelings do you think are still held in your aura? By understanding which emotions you're experiencing, or still holding in your auric field, you can choose to release the resistant or reversed energies and align yourself with the new emotion you want. Our overall aim and focus with EAM is to release the heavy, low vibrational emotions and change our internal emotional set points, which is what we do with Step 5. This creates new imprints in our aura, so that the information fed into the brain via our nervous system is something we'd *choose*, and which supports our journey forward.

Aligned Action

We live in a physical world, which is all energy vibrating in a slower form. While our vision, energy, thoughts, emotions and voice are powerful and contribute to manifesting, we also have to take real-life action. That action has to be congruent to what we want. Sitting and meditating, or visualization alone never works. We also have to 'do' in the physical world to move the dense vibrational frequency too.

This is where *aligned* action comes in. It's different to taking 'massive' action. We'd question the point in any action unless it's guiding you in the direction you want to go. What usually stands in the way of us taking action is incongruent thoughts, beliefs, self doubt and excuses – these are resistance. When you take action from that place, how can it move you in the right direction?

When you use EAM, you consciously choose to release resistance and align your energy, thoughts, beliefs and emotions before you act. This way, you'll be in sync with what you're asking for. Your head, heart and hara will be congruent, which means that the idea, insight or opportunity will present itself.

To create change and transformation on a physical level, we have to take physical action. When you want to manifest a situation or change in your life, make sure your action is congruent with what you say you want.

Your Breath

Your breath is one of THE most important energies in your life. It's known as Da Qi, or the GREAT Qi. Without it, we're unable to last long. Yet, many of us have never learned what it really does, how to breathe properly, or have even paid attention to the way we're breathing in each moment. Many spiritual practices include the power of breath work and EAM is no exception.

Your breath is vitality; it brings clean air and much-needed oxygen into the body. Energetically, it's drawing in a limitless supply of pure potential source energy. Life itself. Your out-breath expels the resistant used energy that is no longer needed by your body. It's sent off into our atmosphere to be transformed and recycled by the earth, plants and trees.

In EAM, we also use the power of our breath to release resistance (Step 4) and to breathe in and re-energize the body using the manifestation power of potential source energy to the new choice, belief, thought or affirmation (Step 5).

Your Powerful Voice

Your voice is also an energy. Sound has energy that can be carried across a room (and if anything like our kids, far beyond!). In Chinese medicine, your tongue is said to be rooted in your heart, so your voice and words have power because they carry heart energy. The vibration of your voice and words also carry far beyond your energy field and contribute to mass consciousness. Vibration and frequency travel. So, if you're speaking words with resistance, you give the words more power, which is sent out and will attract more of a like nature back to you. Use your words wisely.

When talking to others, have you ever noticed that you might say one thing yet somebody hears something completely different? That's because they receive the vibration of your words, instead of the words themselves. So, be mindful of your frequency, the words, what you say, and the language you use.

The power of your voice also perpetuates drama as you give more energy to it. When you talk about what has happened before or what is going wrong, you give more energy to the past or to the situation you're avoiding. In the same way we mentioned above, it gathers momentum. This will energetically 'hold you back' from moving your life forward. In this same way, use your voice to manifest the life you want. The more you talk about what you want and what's coming, the more powerful your manifestation will become, and the quicker it will arrive.

Be Aware of Your Words

The power of your words is especially important when using the Five Steps of EAM, especially when creating your manifesting statements in Step 5. The brain is unable to process negatives so, for example, if we ask you *not* to think of a purple elephant, your brain has to think of one and picture it in order to process it and let it go. In the same way, instead of focusing on what you want to avoid, focus your Step 5 statements on the positive of what you *do* want. For example, changing *'I don't want to fail'* to *'I AM successful in all I do'.*

Your use of words is the secret to manifesting and being successful. When you replace tentative words – 'might', 'may', 'can', 'could' – with the word 'will' there is now certainty that it will happen. 'Try' is another word to avoid, because it signals a lack of commitment. 'But' is another – it unconsciously discounts whatever is said in the sentence prior to the 'but'. We tend to use it as an excuse: *'I'd like to give up smoking but …'* By listening to what we say after the 'but', we can get clearer on what we can release with EAM. For example, *'I'd like to give up smoking but I've tried before and it was too hard'* means you would do EAM on the previous failed attempts and beliefs that it would be hard. When creating your Step 5 statements, use words that are relevant, specific, strong and positive so they connect you energetically to what you want.

The two most powerful words are 'I AM'. Whatever comes after this is a command, a statement to your whole subconscious field. Many religious teachings even teach the power of 'I AM' as a direct command from God, life, source of the universe. These words directly command potential energy. Much of the power of these two little words has been lost through time. They have power to manifest, as it is talking to who you truly are. Yet we make this statement so many times a day, oblivious to the power it has in our lives. We use it to describe almost every feeling or action. When we use the 'I AM' statements in Steps 4 and 5, we do so to clearly command.

It's ONLY YOU who can use this statement about you, and these words will allow you to form an outer reality that is a vibrational match to what you said. So, choose wisely what comes after them.

Use your voice on purpose and become a deliberate and conscious speaker. Choose your words wisely and only give energy to what you want to create.

When you learn how to use EAM in Part Two, you'll use your words to ask the questions to get clarity. By using your voice, you'll also experience a greater shift and release because the power of your voice will resonate through more of your energy field. When you use affirmations after releasing any resistance around it, speak them out loud as often and as frequently as possible. You're retraining your brain, your energy field and heart and sending a powerful frequency out into mass consciousness to bring back what you are asking for. This projects more power and energy to the future you want to create, and voicing it out loud enables it to manifest more quickly.

Our Sixth Sense

Have you ever wondered where you get your inner knowing from? Maybe you've had a moment of insight or intuition before something happens. Like when you think of a friend and suddenly they call.

We know about our five senses – taste, sound, sight, touch and smell. This information is passed to the brain, which sends messages to the body action. Our heart and brain are in constant communication, sending information through nerves, biochemicals, pressure waves and electromagnetic interactions. Remember our heart reads information and sends it *into* the brain before it registers the information from the five senses and *before* it has been able to create chemical messages and send that information out to the body.

The other five senses are taken care of by our eyes, ears, mouth, nose and skin. If that is the case, what is our heart reading? Your energy field. This is our sixth sense! Which is simply your ability to read the subtle changes in energy around you. These changes are in or come in through your energy field. Remember your heart is reading all layers of your auric field and the environment, remembering the 3D map of your subconscious.

We all have six senses – now we have to use them.

When you start using EAM you'll notice your sixth sense will become stronger. As your heart energy becomes clearer, more aligned, you'll notice subtle changes, get more 'intuitive insights', and increase sensitivity to information. We get so excited about this because it challenges what we've all been taught, that the brain controls the heart, when, in fact, it's our heart that rules the house!

You now have an understanding of Qi, flow and how this circulates in your aura, funnels, chakras and meridians. You know your head, heart and hara are sending and receiving information, creating your experience. You understand the power of your vision, energy, thoughts, emotions and taking action to change your life. All of these incredible ways that energy is shaping your life experience. Now, in the rest of this book we want to show you how you can reconnect to that field of potential energy, redirect it and choose where you put it into practice to change your life. Now it's time to look more closely at EAM.

PART TWO

THE ENERGY
ALIGNMENT METHOD

Chapter 5

UNDERSTANDING EAM

Hurray! We're finally here. It's time for the transformation to begin. In this part of the book, we're going to dive into understanding EAM and show you how it works. Learning the Five Steps will give you the tools you need to let go of the past, free yourself from self-sabotage, attract the life you deserve and change anything. Yes, really, *anything*, because it's all just energy.

EAM in a Nutshell

As you saw in this book's introduction, the Energy Alignment Method is a simple, empowering five-step self-help technique, designed to shift energy, thoughts and emotions. Its purpose is to allow you to create the receptive or in-flow state on any subject in your life by releasing any resistant or reversed energy so that you can manifest what you want. The overarching principle is to change your energetic, mental and emotional set points, allowing you to create a new internal reference system. Collectively, we call these set points your *alignment level*. By doing this you bring your head, heart and hara into alignment, raise your vibrational frequency and open up your auric field to master more energy.

EAM enables you to shift stuck energy, and let go of repetitive thoughts and overwhelming emotions. You can release physical or emotional pain, negative feelings, memories and traumatic experiences to be free from stress, feeling overwhelmed and anxious.

By releasing what held you back, you clear your energy field and subconscious. You then choose to create and embody a new vibrational frequency, thought, belief, pattern, emotion or experience that serves *you*. Imagine having the power to find and remove hidden issues, creating a mindset to achieve your dreams and turn them into your reality.

Release what holds you back then create your new reality.

You may be thinking, where do I begin, there are so many issues to work on?! Here's the good news: while we do approach one issue at time, as you implement EAM you'll find a 'tipping point', a ripple effect of increased Qi in flow, that begins to wash over your life like a wave and address other areas too.

We've all felt stuck, fearful and confused about the next steps in life. Perhaps you feel like life is passing you by or you've lost confidence or trust in yourself. Maybe you want to get back on track, to feel passionate and purposeful again, or you feel you're yet to reach your full potential.

As you begin to tune in and master your own energy alignment, with EAM you can instantly transform what you think and how you feel to change any area of your life. You'll create more harmony in your relationships, find your purpose and passion, create self-belief and confidence, and experience more love, happiness, joy and freedom.

We know it may sound too good to be true, yet having seen exactly the same happen with thousands of people around the world, we know it's possible for you, too.

Those who have used it say EAM is so different to other practices they have tried. It's quick, simple and, once you understand the five steps, you can use it on anything. There's no need to relive any drama, because we tap into the subconscious in a painless way. You can make lasting changes in your life because we work with the cause – which is energy – and this frequently works faster than other methods.

We're often asked, '*What exactly does EAM do?*' Here's a simple checklist that gives an overview of how EAM works with your own energy to create a flow state that enables you to manifest what you want:

- **Allows more flow**
  Increases the flow of Qi in your energy field and associated structures into a high-vibrational, expanded, coherent frequency.

- **Creates alignment**
  The increased flow creates synchronization and communication in our aura, chakras, meridians and their associated functions.

- **Transforms your reality**
  By changing the potential energy in our field, we become a vibrational match to what we choose, which changes our life and the reality we observe.

- **Enables shifts in all forms**
  Releases all forms of resistances or reversals and creates new imprints in all potential formations within our energy system.

- **Works on all levels at all points in time**
  Works synchronistically on all seven levels of our life experience, changing the energy connected to past, present and future events in the energy field. This creates changes in our past, present and future experience, too.

- **Gives you motivation and energy**
  The coherent state creates more drive – you have more motivation to get up and go, and more energy flow to direct to different areas of your life.

- **Gets you out of your own way**
  We are often the one thing standing in the way of changing our life. Once we know that it's what's in our energy that creates the challenges, we can get ourselves out the way of our own success.

- **Changes our set points**
  Studies have shown that with the use of methods such as EAM our brain literally rewires itself. We can unwire set points or pathways, disassociating particular thoughts, memories and emotions. And by creating new experiences in our energy, thoughts and emotions (Step 5), we create new neural pathways, rewiring the brain. These set points become our new internal references.

- **Creates new patterns**
  Step 5 allows us to create new positive energetic patterns in our whole energy system, in different auric layers, and change the electromagnetic messages we send out.

- **Brings about synchronicity between heart and brain**
  Coherence creates better neurological communication between our heart, brain and endocrine system. When in flow, this is how we create positive emotions and thoughts and use our intuition.

- **Creates a prayer state**
  It has been proven that saying positive affirmations and prayers out loud actually creates a coherence in our energy. While prayer is often related to religious practice, by using EAM and affirming our new positive intentions, we create a prayer-like state. Remember the power of our voice by creating the new statement is a declaration of our intention, like a prayer.

So, what does this mean for you? It's all of the benefits we learned about when exploring the state of flow in Part One. Among many benefits, you'll:

- create more positive emotions for longer periods of time
- reset everything in your energy
- naturally attract more into your life
- have better mental and emotional bounce back
- become more adaptive to change
- be better able to deal with traumatic events
- create more positive new experiences
- reduce adrenal and cortisol levels and create endorphins
- resolve the stress phase and promote the healing phase

As I've said before, once you recognize that everything is energy and that you can change your energy, thoughts and emotions with EAM, you can and will change your life.

When to Use EAM

When should you use EAM? The answer is simple … all the time, all day, every day. Whenever an opportunity presents itself. There are also some simple clues that indicate when EAM would be particularly beneficial. Remember, it's about more than releasing resistance. Use it when life feels good, to create more receptivity. When you use EAM, you feel better about life right now *and* in the future. By getting in alignment, you're creating the future you want. Can you see how you can use it everyday? This is where the magic of EAM lies.

Here are a few clues that tell you it would be good to do some EAM. Use it when:

- energy is low or you're in a bad mood
- noticing resistant thoughts or feelings
- hearing yourself say or write down beliefs that need working on
- you feel ill, tired or run down
- feeling stuck, lost or like you've hit a wall
- judging yourself or others
- dragged down by other people
- feeling confused
- life feels like it's going wrong, or you're unable to change it
- there are decisions to be made and you feel unsure what to do
- noticing self-sabotaging behaviours
- you're pushing to change situations or people so that you feel better
- you feel like giving up
- you find yourself in pusher, puller or protector roles (we'll talk more about these in the next chapter)

- creating or manifesting something in your life
- you're in a good mood and want to feel even better

These are just a few of the hundreds of ways you can recognize it's time for a bit of EAM. Get in the habit of using it whenever you feel resistance. You'll feel when there's something to release, and then instantly be able to clear it before it grows into something more.

The easiest answer is to pay attention to how you feel at every moment. If you feel out of alignment, do the Five Steps. If you're in alignment, do more of Step 5. You'll soon feel the magic and will be using it all the time!

Limitations of EAM

EAM is a powerful self-help method, which can enable many shifts and changes, and it's primarily used as a preventative tool to stop you from getting to critical points in your physical, mental or emotional health. We are all responsible for ourselves, our life and our health, and there are times when we would recommend you refrain from using EAM, and seek professional help, support and attention instead.

For example, refrain from using EAM when there's a medical emergency, which requires attention from a physician or other health care provider. In such cases, please contact the relevant services. You can use EAM to help manage the pain and symptoms as well as seeking medical assistance. If someone is having a psychological episode, such as a mental or nervous breakdown, or is feeling very low and having suicidal thoughts, please seek support from the appropriate medical professionals. EAM can be used to calm, and to provide comfort by releasing resistant thoughts and emotions and aligning to positive statements, however you still need those services.

Your Powerful Sway

One of the key components of EAM is a form of muscle testing known as 'the sway'. It's a simple biofeedback method to determine where stressors or areas of resistance are held in all layers of our energy field. Through muscle-testing questions, and monitoring of the answers, we can access information from our subconscious. To sway, it's best to stand with your feet hip-width apart and ask simple 'yes' or 'no' answer questions. Your body will usually sway forward for a 'yes' answer and backward for a 'no'.

The sway is a physiological response sent via tiny nerves that create a micro-muscle movement, known as an ideomotor response. On a physiological level, we're working with our autonomic nervous system that controls the electrical input and output of messages. This system knows what's happening everywhere in our body all of the time – it monitors information from the inside (our body) and the outside (our environment) and responds accordingly. Your nervous system is adjusting your physiology all the time. For example, when you're embarrassed, you become hot and sweaty. You never consciously think, *'Oh yes, better start sweating'*! Your body does this without any input from your conscious mind.

This same part of the autonomic nervous system monitors our electromagnetic energy field. In this case, it creates a motor (physical muscular) response to what we're thinking, feeling or picking up energetically. By using the sway with EAM, we can get a 'yes' or 'no' response to what's happening on every level of our energy field.

Your body is constantly responding to your senses. The sway is reading your sixth sense, meaning it is reading the energy field and environment.

The Importance of the Sway

In EAM, we use the sway to get real-time feedback on what's happening in our energy field. By using this process we can understand subconscious information, which would otherwise be inaccessible to our conscious awareness. The sway is used in multiple ways throughout the Five Steps of EAM.

Why do we use the sway instead of what's in our head? Because the sway enables us to bypass conscious thinking to identify unconscious thoughts, beliefs and energy about any subject. We may do things we never consciously admit to, because they may be perceived as wrongful, dishonest or impolite, for example. Our ego might say, *'I am not jealous. That's not me. I am too nice to be jealous'*. Yet, there are unconscious hidden feelings that say otherwise. If we only used our conscious awareness, we'd limit our transformation because we edit ourselves based on our current awareness, beliefs and filters. Our consciousness is an incomplete picture. We need to access our subconscious, too. By asking the sway, you bypass the mind, access the energy field and understand what's truly holding you back vibrationally. This means we can transform the real issues that we may be unaware of.

Ask your sway to get true answers from your subconscious.

Similarly, you may ask if you can use a pendulum or another dowsing device to get answers to your questions? Firstly you have all the answers you need inside of *you*. Why use something external when your body is giving you answers all the time? You can use the sway anywhere. We've found it to be more accurate than a pendulum, which can be easily influenced by your thinking. With the sway, you *feel* your emotions and shifts in your frequency, so you become more aware of your flow state. We want you to fall so in love with your sway, to understand the power you hold and listen to the guidance you've had inside you all along. Our energy field holds all the information, so why look elsewhere. The only person who has the true answer to what is happening for you is you. When using a pendulum you have no physiological or emotional feedback to connect you to what's happening in your energy field. The direction of your sway also gives you important information.

How to Get a Good Sway

The ultimate aim is to get you to a point where you trust your sway, where you're in tune with yourself and your vibration. At the beginning, it may feel a little clunky but follow this advice and you'll soon get the hang of it. If you're familiar with kinesiology, you know about testing for a strong or weak response from your body. As you use EAM, you'll notice that sways differ. Sometimes, you have a strong pull forward ('yes' response) or backward ('no' response) and sometimes the sways can be gentle or almost imperceptible. If your sways feel small or weak to begin with, this is often because our energy channels are stuck, or your funnel is closed – the more you use EAM to free up your energy field the stronger it becomes. The strength of the sway can also tell you how 'true' or 'false' a statement is to you. It may make you fall forward or throw you backward sometimes, please take care! So how do we get a good sway?

Be in the Right Space

There are many different sources in our environment that can stop a 'good sway'. Unknowingly to you, they can put your body into a weak, reversed or resistant state. They affect more than your sway, too; imagine what they do to your energy *all the time*. Here's a quick list:

- being tired
- medication
- alcohol
- sugar
- caffeine
- your diet
- technology
- personal hygiene, cleaning products
- particular environments
- other people

You can ask the sway if any of these are affecting you. Ironically, they may stop you from getting the right answer! We'll show you what to do with that shortly.

When using the sway, make sure you're fully hydrated. If you can, be barefoot and, if possible, outside in the grass or at least on the ground floor of your house to earth or ground any resistant energy. If you have any trouble swaying, jump up and down, go for a little run, lie outside, dance or sing to reset your energy. These things aren't essential, but can be helpful when starting to use the sway as they help clear your energy field.

Have the Right Stance

If you're holding your body locked, with a tight clenched fist, a stiff back, your shoulders up around your ears and the back of your knees locked, does that feel open, relaxed and ready to receive? If you're holding tension in your body, it will prevent you from getting a clear answer from the sway. To start, stand tall with your feet hip-width apart, close your eyes, and take a nice deep breath. Consciously relax the back of your knees and hips, and open your hands so they're by your sides.

Remain Objective

Yes, you can influence your sway, forward or backward, if you choose. With EAM, remember to remain objective, your only intention is to get a truthful answer from your energy. Often we're invested in getting a particular answer, then feel disappointed when we get another. This, too, gives you some insight and places to explore with EAM.

You'll begin to know when you have a real sway as opposed to one you've 'encouraged', as it has a different feeling. The push or pull comes from inside without any thought or conscious awareness of the question you're asking. In the same way, if you keep asking the same question you may get different answers at different times – remember your sway is a 'messenger' telling you what your energy is vibrating. If you change your thoughts or emotions about something, the sway will change.

Be Specific and Ask the Right Questions

The words and meanings you use can determine the outcome of your sway, so be specific with your questions. For example, in response to the question 'Am I feeling angry?', the sway might tell you 'no', because right now, no, you are not connected to anger. If you ask the sway, 'Do I feel angry when I think about what Bob did to me last week, when he said my bum looked big?' then you might get a different answer.

Your sway is also influenced by your beliefs. You may ask, 'Do I believe I SHOULD take this job?' and sway 'yes' forward, yet if you ask, 'Do I want to take this job?', you may sway backward. Similar question, different answers. You may believe you *should* take the job because it will provide safety, security and money. Yet deep inside, you know that taking the job would break your heart and destroy your soul because it's taking you away from your passion. Do you see how important it is to be specific about the questions?

Be clear and simply ask questions you want to ask.

We recommend leaving out words like 'should' or 'ought to' from your questions. Instead, ask, 'Do I want … ?', or 'Would I like … ?' or 'Is it for my highest good?' If you're specific with your questions, it will enable you to understand what to release and what to align to.

Practising Your Sway

Now, up on your feet! Let's start you using your sway. You need to learn to trust it. Here are a few suggestions to enable you to get started; ask the questions two or three times to see what answers you get. Make sure you're familiar with the steps above for a good sway.

Stand with your feet hip-width apart, relax your body and close your eyes. Pick up different foods or objects in your home one time at a time – items to which you've no emotional attachment. Ask out loud, '*Is this good for me?*' and see if your body pulls forward (yes) or back (no). If you find a product which makes you sway backward you can ask again for each individual ingredient. This may give you clues as to substances that affect your energy. See which ones you go forward and backward on.

Once you have confidence with inanimate objects, you can use simple statements. Say these out loud then say the opposite; for example, I would say '*My name is Yvette*', and I would expect to sway forward. Then if I said, '*My name is Frank*', I would expect to sway backward. Carry out the following, with truthful and untruthful statements:

- My name is
- My date of birth is
- My mother's name is
- My father's name is

These are really helpful as long as there's no energetic attachment to those subjects. For example, if you have a negative relationship with your mum, when you ask her name there may be something that affects your sway. If you've tried these questions and your sway is still affected sometimes you need to sleep. Your body works on the circadian clock and it may be that you're using the sway during a time in the day when your particular energy flow is at its lowest.

It's usual to be a little uncertain of your sway when you begin using it. Just start with simple questions or statements to get confidence in your sway. You'll soon get to know a real sway. If you feel your sway is being unclear, this is usually an indication of an energy reversal. Follow the steps on page 158 to clear this.

Chapter 6

THE FIVE STEPS OF EAM

Now that you understand the sway, it's time for us to finally share the Five Steps of EAM with you. (I bet you thought we'd never get here!) This chapter explains exactly how to use EAM by taking you through the Five Steps in detail. Read the whole chapter in full before putting it into practice, so you fully understand what we're doing with each step. Here they are:

Step 1 – You Ask	You'll ask your energy field a question
Step 2 – You Move	Your sway will respond 'yes' or 'no'
Step 3 – You Experience	Understand how the challenge is affecting your energy
Step 4 – You Transform	Say the release statement to shift the resistance or reversal
Step 5 – You Manifest	Create a new thought, belief, pattern, emotion or experience

The Five Steps allow you to explore any issue or challenge about a subject, situation or person, or to amplify an existing positive experience or situation you wish to manifest. Whatever topic you are working on, EAM is primarily a self-help tool, meaning that you can do so much for yourself!

We'll introduce you to the basic principles of EAM, so you have the skills to approach any reversal or resistance and transform the energy into the receptive (in-flow) state.

Remember, you can use EAM to amplify an existing flow state to a higher frequency. It's best to complete all of the Five Steps together about a subject to really feel the benefit of it.

EAM's power is in its simplicity once you understand the Five Steps. When you start using EAM, focus on the energy, thoughts, beliefs or emotions you feel about a particular subject. There's no need to begin exploring anything else. Once you master those, you can begin implementing EAM in other areas, many of which are outside the possibilities in this book.

The purpose of everything within EAM is to align your whole energy field and raise your frequency. In Step 4 and Step 5 we use powerful statements to command our energy. It's useful to understand the meanings. The words *'in all forms'* represent *all* of the types of resistance, reversals, imprints, blobs, rubble, etc, and various vibrations you feel in your energy. *'On all levels'* means all levels of our life experience, aura, energy systems and vibrations in the field of energy. *'At all points in time'* means past, present, future and concurrent lifetimes. This is why transformations with EAM can take minutes (rather than seconds), because we cover it all at once, when you know the Five Steps.

Do it all at once, all forms, levels and points in time!

No matter what has happened in your past, using EAM can free you from whatever holds you back. You can step into your power and create the life you want, dream of and deserve.

Let's take a look at the Five Steps of EAM in detail, so you understand what they are, why we do each one, and how to put this into practice for yourself.

Step 1 - Ask

In Step 1, we ask ourselves (our energy field) a question, which is best said aloud. Think of a subject, situation or personal relationship you'd like to explore. It could be something you know is a challenge or something you want to align to manifesting. The questions you ask will allow you to understand whether your Qi is in a receptive, resistance or reversal state about that subject. By asking our energy field, we're asking the question to all levels of our subconscious – ultimately, we're speaking to our heart, which is reading our energy systems, structures and functions all at once.

With Step 1, we get clarity on our issue through questioning. This enables us to bypass our conscious awareness and access our subconscious. By saying it aloud, we engage the energetic power of our voice, the vibration resonates with our energy field, and we get a more truthful answer because it comes from the heart – it's more powerful than asking silently in your head.

This is where we will first use the sway. Begin by standing with your feet hip-width apart, knees relaxed, eyes closed, hands by your side. Take a deep breath and relax. Then ask yourself a question that can give you a simple 'yes' or 'no' answer. (We'll look at how you actually sway in Step 2.) Keep it simple when you first start working on an issue.

Depending on your chosen subject, you (your body and energy) may approach it in different ways. When you bring it to mind, the subject may present primarily in your thoughts, or in your emotions, or in the way you 'feel' your energy. You might feel a sensation in your heart, or notice a belief or thought, or feel an emotion like anger. These are the different approaches:

1. What Is Happening to Your Energy?

Before you even ask your first question, when you think about the issue, what happens in your energy? Do you feel heavy or light? Sick in your stomach? Does it make you feel like you're walking in mud or skipping on air? Then, based on what you're sensing with your energy, you can start and ask your sway a question like:

> *'Does it make me feel heavy and pulled back when I think about _____?'*
> or
> *'Is this heavy and pulled back feeling related to _____?'*

2. What Beliefs or Thoughts Do You Have?

If it creates no physiological response, look at the thoughts or beliefs you have around the subject. You may want to write them down or listen to yourself explaining it to someone else. For instance, do you hold a belief that you aren't good enough to get that job? Then you could ask your sway a Step 1 question like:

> *'Do I believe I am not good enough to get that job?'*
> or
> *'Do I think I will fail at that interview?'*

3. What Emotions Do You Feel?

If what you experience is something other than a belief or feeling, it may be an emotion. These are different to the two kinds of energies described above. Emotions are ones you recognize quite easily, such as anger, anxiety, happiness, love and sadness. If you've identified an emotion for yourself, you could ask a Step 1 question like:

'Do I feel angry that James didn't do what I asked him to?'
or
'Do I hold any emotions of anger when I think about _____?

4. Check Your Alignment

You can use the Five Steps to amplify an existing receptive state or check if you're in alignment with something you want to manifest. You may feel no resistance at all or already feel positive about the subject. This is a powerful way to ensure you're in alignment with your manifestations.

You could ask a Step 1 question like:

'Am I in alignment/flow/ready to receive/create/ experience _____?'

When people begin using EAM they often say, *'Well I already know what I am feeling, so can I just do Step 4?'* We would suggest no, because what you *think* is the issue may be different to what it actually is in your vibrational field. If you skip Step 1, you'll miss the specificity and clarity of exactly what you need to work on with answers from your sway. This is part of the power of EAM. By asking the right questions, you discover the real resistance in your energy. This means that when you get to Step 4, you can transform the actual underlying reason.

It's precisely because we get to this level of specificity by asking the questions in Steps 1 and 2 that people report such rapid shifts with EAM. You may find yourself asking several questions, cycling between Steps 1 and 2 for clarity before you can move to Steps 3, 4 and 5. That is perfectly normal and part of the process.

The exception to this is if you're experiencing something highly intense or emotional. In those circumstances, start your practice at Step 3.

Step 2 – Move

In Step 2, your body will sway in response to the question. Your heart reads your energy field, including your aura layers, physical body, chakras, meridians, thoughts, emotions and other imprints in your energy. This information is fed back through our autonomic nervous system, to create the ideomotor and neuromuscular response, which we know as the sway.

We use the sway at Step 2 to tune into the exact issue. There's no need to be consciously aware of every resistance to transform, although at times it helps to piece together a puzzle that may have been invisible. The sway allows you to get a deep insight into what's happening in your energy field. As your frequency increases, your intuition will too, so you'll need to use your sway less. By using our physiology, we can see and feel what's happening in our energy field and get access to answers previously held and left unknown in your subconscious.

Understand Your Sway in Step 2

In Step 2, your body will respond to the question. A typical sway forward is a 'yes' and a sway backward is a 'no'. If you get a no to something you think you have a resistance or reversal to, move back to Step 1. Ask the question again by changing the words to get more clarity, or consider that you might be experiencing something different to what you originally thought.

The purpose of Step 2 is to clarify exactly what's happening in your energy field. It's normal to repeat Step 1 and 2 a couple of times until you get a yes, then you move to Step 3. If you experience no resistance or reversals, and want to check your alignment to something you want to create, you would ask, *'Am I in alignment with …?'*, to see if you're in the receptive state on a subject; then you can move to Step 5.

We share more on how to shift a reversal on page 158.

Here are a few guide notes you may find useful when getting used to your sway.

- **If your sway doesn't work**

  Energetically, you may be operating in survival mode and at a vibrationally low frequency. This is the reversed energy state, and means you'll often find it difficult to sway. You can use EAM to support you, to get the sway to work. One way would be to simply use Step 4 (the release statement, see p. 145) on your sway being ineffective. The other would be to begin exploring what created this reversed state. This can be difficult, as your sway is unable to provide clues where to look. If you're unable to sway, use EAM anyway to work on releasing the reversal by describing what it feels like in your energy.

  These problems are common and also very easy to shift and transform when you apply the Five Steps as suggested. At the beginning, because your energy may be slower, it may take several sessions to raise your vibration or understand which questions to ask to release it. This is perfectly normal and you can always ask for guidance. This is where our free support group, courses, or the support of an EAM mentor would be highly beneficial to get you started.

- **Using your sway to make decisions**

  We hear this from people a lot: *'My sway says I SHOULD or SHOULDN'T do it'*. Please remember, your sway is an indication of what's in your energy field right now. If you hold fear or a negative emotion about something, that is the answer your sway will tell you. To get a true answer from your sway, first release any resistance or reversal (see Step 4), otherwise it influences the response. When you're in alignment, with no incongruent energy about that subject, ask the question and the answer will be truthful – you'll get a clear 'yes' or a clear 'no'. When you do, it means your energy, thoughts and emotions are in sync, and you can use them to guide your actions.

- **It all changes**

  Let me briefly clarify, a sway forward is *usually* a 'yes' and backward is *usually* a 'no'. We say 'usually' because one of the clearest signs that we have an energy reversal is that our sway suddenly becomes difficult to read. The answers often change position, meaning your 'yes' becomes backward and your 'no' becomes forward. Argh! If this happens, you need to follow the process for clearing a reversal, as outlined later in this chapter (see p. 158).

- **Standing still or going in circles**

  If this happens, it could be that you need to ask a clearer question. It can also be another sign of a reversal, so follow the steps to clear this. It's also a reversal when you sway from side to side, or if you move in a circle instead of swaying clearly backward or forward. This can get a bit confusing. Is it a 'real' yes? Or a 'fake' caused by a reversal? You'll get the hang of it. A simple way to check is by asking what your name is (assuming you've no reversal around your name). It's often quicker to just follow the steps and release the resistance anyway.

- **Swaying back and forth**
  Swaying back and forth while doing Step 4 or Step 5 is a sign your body is moving its energy. You may also sway as you say a statement. This means that it's very true (forward) or false (backward) for you. You may sway before you've even verbalized your question because your energy knows the answer before you're consciously aware.

- **Sways from different parts of the body**
  You may notice that the sway comes from different places such as your heart, between your shoulders, your stomach or solar plexus, or below your belly button. All of these are normal, so trust that it's a yes (forward) or no (backward) sway.

- **Swaying sitting or lying down**
  When you first learn EAM we teach you to sway standing up. It's one of the easiest ways to muscle test because gravity enables the movement, so you get a clearer signal. However, you can sway standing up or from anywhere that has a pivot. If you can sit on the edge of a chair, see if you can sway from your hips. You'll feel the same push and pull of energy between your heart and shoulder blades. Once you master this, you can use EAM anywhere – while travelling, sitting on the sofa or even on the loo! If sitting unaided is a challenge, you can also sway from your neck and use your head. You'll nod forward or backward, so long as the back of your chair allows free movement of your head. You can also sway

lying down! This is a great one to master; it feels like a pull upward or that you're being pushed down if you're lying flat on your back. These are particularly useful for people with health or mobility issues, who may lack strength, or are bed-bound. Try these out for yourself so you can use EAM any and everywhere.

As a general rule, be specific when you've asked a broad question with diverse possible answers, for example: *'Do I have resistance to money?'* That is a huge topic with multiple elements. So, your sway could be answering something that may be both resistant *and* reversed. This will create a confusing sway. Be more specific with your questions and explore them with clarifying questions at Step 3.

When you first start using EAM, you may need to be patient, as your body may be slow to respond. Give it a moment or two. Your sway can also be imperceptible. If so, go back to page 118 and check out how to get a good sway.

If your sway remains confusing on a particular subject, you probably have a reversal, in which case it's best to move straight to Step 4 and clear this reversal as a general release statement before continuing.

If you ask the question and find no resistance to a subject, situation or person you're manifesting, double check by asking clarifying questions on the same topic in Step 3. If nothing comes up, you can skip Step 4 and move to Step 5 and align.

Once you've identified a clear 'yes' at Step 2 to something that is a resistance or reversal ready to be released, meaning you sway forward, then you can move onto Step 3.

Step 3 – Experience

Step 3 is when you 'experience', meaning that you want to assess how the resistances or reversals around that subject affect your energy field. We all interpret energy differently, which means they show up for us all in different ways, too. At this point, you're still standing, with eyes closed, and tuning into and interpreting your sway and how your energy feels.

With multiple approaches to Step 3, we vary the exercise depending on your learning style; or how the resistance or reversal expresses in your energy field. For example, people who are kinaesthetic communicate best by feel or touch – they might describe resistance as a feeling or sensation, such as a heavy dark ball in their heart. This is also a powerful way to interpret sway when you experience no clear emotion, just a sensation.

Other people may be logical, and like to use numbers and systems. There is an approach to clarifying that uses numbers (see p. 136), which is also useful when people are stuck in their head or unable to feel anything in their energy. Some people may learn visually and see pictures in their mind's eye, such as a brick wall restricting their path, to indicate how something is affecting them. All of these can be applied to Step 3.

Part of the transformational process is having a conscious understanding or realization of what, why or how something occurred, and this step gives conscious clarity on what's standing in your way. What is your current experience or level of resistance on this subject? Remember your voice is powerful. By verbalizing and naming feelings at this step, you tune into the frequency and put conscious meaning and common language to something intangible. You'll also gain a greater insight into how it affects your energy or life experience; you'll get more specific descriptions to use and have a marker of the resistance or reversal before transforming it in Step 4. This will help you know when it has gone.

Five Ways to Apply Step 3

Step 3 brings the state of your energy into your conscious awareness, so you can work out what to transform at Step 4. Here are five key exercises to help you approach this.

1. Energy
The easiest EAM approach is to describe **what happens to your energy** when you focus on a particular subject. Simply ask yourself, '*What happens to my energy when I think about ___?*' Describe it in the same way that we looked at in Step 1, for example, does it feel heavy or light? Do you feel tired or drained? There are lots of ways that imprints in your energy field can affect you. Defining them here makes it easier to transform with Step 4.

The body always sends us messages about our imprints and disturbances. What you're feeling as sensations are the resistant or reversed energy that you're unable to name or describe.

The reason we begin with noticing our energy is because many people are generally disconnected from their body. As a society, we've learned to ignore or push aside these very clear signals that something is going on. Tuning in enables you to gain a greater sense of self-awareness. As you grow with EAM, you'll begin to notice changes in your energy field *before* it gets out of alignment.

To focus on feeling your energy, stand with your eyes closed and think about the situation, memory or person that you feel you need to work on. Pay attention to what's happening in your body. You may notice feelings straight away, or you may need to work methodically and focus on each part, from head to toes, to notice changes. You may feel the energy inside or outside of you – it could be a pressure, heaviness or tension, or feel like holes or gaps in your energy. It can help to define the feeling as an inanimate object. You can identify it verbally or ask the question of yourself or the sway:

- What colour is it? Can you 'see' one in your mind's eye?
- What size is it? For example, is it the size of a tennis ball or a rugby ball?
- What shape is it? Can you describe it as a square, circle, triangle or a weird blob?
- Is it hard or soft?
- Is it still or moving?
- Is moving fast or slow? How does it move?
- Is it inside or outside of your physical body?
- Where is it located?
- Does it feel like another object, for example, a knife or spear?

The answers will help you to formulate a statement to release the resistance with Step 4 of EAM. For example, if you're feeling stressed out about work, when you close your eyes it might feel like there's a hard, spiky tennis ball inside your stomach. The ball feels like it's spinning and is half inside and half outside of your body, like it's bursting to get out. You would then use this description in Step 4 to transform along the lines of,

'I AM ready to transform this hard, spiky tennis ball that feels like it bursting to get out of my stomach, when I think about work. I release this from my energy in all forms, on all levels, at all points in time.'

2. Numbers

Numbers are very useful to quantify something you're unable to feel. They are also a finite way of ensuring that you've released all of the resistance. They work with our thoughts, beliefs or patterns, and number of emotions we are carrying in our aura. You seldom need to be specific with the numbers that you discover with this step – they are simply a guideline to represent how many repetitions of that thought, pattern, feeling, experience, belief, etc, you need to transform in Step 4.

By using the sway to define the number that relates to your subject, you can see when you've cleared it down to zero. This is very empowering. People who are more logical or find it hard to define feelings or energy in the body find this useful. By using numbers, you can also group many different thoughts, feelings or beliefs at once, speeding up the releasing process instead of having to define each one. You can then measure how many you need to transform with Step 4 and release them all very quickly.

There are lots of ways you can work with numbers in EAM. For example, you can ask the sway:

> *'Do I have more than 100 beliefs that (insert the belief, thought or pattern)?'*

The sway will give you a 'yes' or 'no'. If it's a yes, ask again and go up in number.

> *'Do I have more than 1,000 beliefs that _____?'*

This time the sway may say 'no', so you know that it's less than 1,000. You can then ask if the number is more or less than halfway between that number and the previous one.

> *'Do I have more than 500 beliefs that _____?'*

Keep using this process up and down until you get in the region of the number. Remember, you rarely need to be exact.

You then use this same process to release the resistance with Step 4 and count back down the number of resistances until you get to 0.

When using numbers, it may take more than one or two rounds of repeating Step 4 to release the resistances or reversals – this is totally normal. The numbers help us to see what we've released. Use them as a measure or guide to know if you need to repeat Step 4. For example, if you initially find 1,000 beliefs, use Step 4 to reduce it down to 100 the first time. Then repeat Step 4 to reduce it further. Then, you might ask the sway and find it's been reduced to 50. Repeat, and you might find it's down to 10. Continue until it gets to 0.

However, if it gets stuck and the number stays the same, you may have an energy reversal to clear. By using the numbers, you're able to identify how many of those remaining are energy reversals, and specifically go in and work on each individual one (see p. 136), so you can clear Step 4. The numbers allow you to be specific and ensure a complete release.

Finally, forget about comparing yourself to others. You may identify numbers in the millions while other people only have a few hundred. People process information in different ways; it's held in your energy differently too, so numbers are irrelevant. They're simply a measure of what *you* hold in *your* energy. Either way, it only matters that you get it down to zero.

3. Emotions

We explored our emotional scale in Chapter 4 (see p. 97). You can use it as a guide to ask your sway which specific emotions you're feeling and how many times you've experienced them. This is a powerful tool, which enables you to work through particular situations or how you feel about other people. It's your reference guide; the scale enables you to explore other emotions connected to these feelings.

Often, we're unable to name emotions connected to a situation. Our thoughts can be clouded and emotions muddied by our perception. They can be confused by the way our neural networks have bound information together, or we might use different words to explain emotions. Often we hide the emotions we feel, or deny we have them. Remember, emotions are vibrations of a particular frequency; by using the scale, you know where your emotional frequencies are on that subject, situation or person. Remember, too, your heart is more powerful than your mind. Emotions have a greater impact on your life experience than your thoughts, whether you're consciously aware of them or not.

To use the emotional scale, ensure you have a copy of it to hand (you can use the one on page 97). Ask the sway which emotion you feel when thinking of the subject, situation or person you're working on. Start at the bottom of the scale and ask about each emotion, writing down the ones you sway 'yes' to. For example, you may have fear, jealousy and anger on that topic.

Ask your sway:

'Do I feel fear when I think about _____?'
or
'Do I feel jealous when I think about _____?'

The sway will answer 'yes' or 'no'.

If yes, there are two ways to then use this. Either use the energy approach – for example, what it feels like in your energy – or use the numbers process to discern how many times you've repeated that emotion, as described on page 136.

Again, use your findings here to formulate the statement for Step 4. It might look something like this:

'I AM ready to transform these 473 feelings of fear when thinking about my new job. I release it from my energy in all forms, on all levels, at all points in time.'
or
'I AM ready to release this dark, heavy bubbling feeling of fear in my hara when I think about my new job. I release it from my energy in all forms, on all levels, at all points in time.'

Please remember, we can hold resistance to *all* emotions, even those like empowerment, happiness, confidence or love. These can be connected to any subject, situation or person – you may have resistances around showing love to a particular person, for example. This is especially useful to know when it comes to Step 5, as you may have a resistance to asking for what you want and that will hinder your ability to manifest with it.

4. Clarifying Questions

You can have a lot of fun asking your sway weird and crazy questions. This is useful for finding out when a particular issue began for you; or when it's hard to define an emotion; or if you're unable to describe it with feelings or numbers, yet you know it's an issue in your life. These questions allow you to get specific.

The list of possible questions is endless, let's begin with a few simple ones. These questions will be especially useful to you when working on releasing an energy reversal (p. 158). You may wish to come back here and work through them. Avoid getting bogged down digging in the past. Use the questions to get specific; once you have the answer, move on and transform it with Step 4.

These questions will guide you to find the specific resistance or start point, which resolves all the connected resistances that follow after that. It could be from this life, from your time in the womb, or from a past life (if you believe in those). For example, you could ask:

- Was it this life?
- Was it in the womb?
- Was it a past life?
- What age was I?
- Do I need to know more?

This is similar to the numbers process we used above. Use the sway to identify your age at the time the resistance or reversal began. So, you'd ask questions like:

- Was I younger than 10, 20, 30?

When your sway answers 'yes' or 'no', work up or down accordingly until you find the age. When you get a yes, you may want to explore some more questions. For example, if you were 5 years old, you were probably going to school rather than work. You may remember something at that age or a significant life event. Ask your sway if they're connected:

- Was it when _____?

or

- Who else was involved?
  Was it my mum/dad/brother/sister/aunt/uncle/teacher/ friend?

The sway will give you yes or no answers to these questions to get clarity. This may lead you on to more questions like:

- Was it something I/they heard?
- Was it something I/they said?
- Was it something I/they did?
- Was it something I/they believed?

Once you have these clarifying answers you can ask a more direct question to be sure. For example, if you'd been working on a belief that '*I AM not good enough*' you could then ask:

- Was it that I heard my mum and dad talking about me and I believed that they thought I wasn't good enough?

If yes, your Step 4 release statement would look something like:

> **'I AM ready to transform the belief that I AM not good enough, created at the age 5 when I overheard my mum and dad talking about me in the kitchen. I release it from my energy in all forms on all levels, at all points in time.'**

You can usually skip this level of detail; simply by identifying the age you were, then transform the resistance or reversal.

If it was in the womb, you can ask which month of pregnancy it was, again using numbers. You can also ask:

- Was it something my mum heard/said/felt/thought/believed or experienced?
- Was it something I heard/felt/thought/believed or experienced?

Then work on releasing it with Step 4. Your statement would look something like this:

> *'I AM ready to release this feeling of fear that my mum had, when she was three months pregnant with me. I release this from my energy in all forms, on all levels, at all points in time.'*

If it was in a past life you can explore some questions like:

- Which past life was it? For example, five past lives ago.
- Were you a woman/man/girl/boy?
- What age were you?
- Were you married/single/a child?
- What other important relationships did you have?
- Did something happen to you or someone you love?

Then maybe explore the circumstances of what happened. Your Step 4 statement may look something like this:

> *'I AM ready to release this energy REVERSAL from five past lives ago, when I was a man, aged 35, and my wife was kidnapped and I never saw her again. I release this from my energy in all forms, on all levels, at all points in time.'*

We'll be honest, these questions may seem a bit 'out there' when you first begin, especially if this work is new to you. The intention is never to conflict with your belief system. However, having worked with thousands of people, we've seen that many of our biggest challenges are in these areas. It's all just energy and another line of questioning, which may enable you to uncover different resistances and reversals that are holding you back right now. Try it out for yourself.

5. Visualization

Some people are more visual. For Step 3, you can also use pictures, which you may see in your mind's eye or imagination. When you close your eyes and think of that topic, you may create a visual representation of what that resistance or reversal is like for you. Describe the picture. For example, you may feel trapped by life. When you close your eyes, you see that you're in a prison and it's surrounding you on all sides. If so, your Step 4 statement would look something like this:

> *'I AM ready to transform this feeling of being trapped inside a prison on all sides when I think about my life. I release this from my energy, in all forms, on all levels, at all points in time.'*

When you release, you'll check or notice if the visualization still looks the same, has changed, or has gone before moving to Step 5. For example, the prison walls may have gone and you're now standing in a field.

So, those are a few ways that you can explore Step 3, accounting for a variety of learning styles and ways of reading or interpreting information in our energy field. As you learn more about EAM, you'll discover ever more ways to approach situations, all of them building on these basic skills.

Now you've completed Step 3 and assessed your energy, what it is and why and how it occurred, you're ready to move to Step 4.

Step 4 – Transform

In Step 4, we say a simple statement to transform the energy from a resistance or reversal into the receptive or in-flow state. When our energy is free-flowing, we can direct it toward the outcome we'd like. Step 4 is about releasing the old paradigm, so we can move into the new. By releasing what's held in our energy field, we change our observation, which changes our reality, through choice.

You can use the same simple statement using the powerful 'I AM' words to command your energy to transform, varying the wording depending on the topic you're working on. The words we say at Step 4 change the way we think and feel, and change any imprints that may be held in our energy field.

Most other energy or healing modalities fall into one of two camps. Either they focus on the release, never including a positive manifestation step, or they focus on the positive step and do nothing to release when, in fact, both are vital. If you focus only on the release you go into a low-energy state leaving a gap in your biofield as your body goes into healing – this can make you feel down or low in energy. And if you focus only on manifesting without releasing, you're still pushing against your own resistances or reversals in your energy.

Remember, if you have trouble with your sway working you can do Steps 4 and 5 anyway – describe what and how you're feeling or thinking and go with that. It will still free up Qi and help your sway to work, even if you have to repeat Step 4 a few times.

You've heard us say that your voice is your heart. In Chinese medicine, the heart is the emperor, so any time you use your voice it's literally giving a command. The words we use at this step are commanding your life force to follow the actions.

In Step 4, we always use the same statement, including any adaptations for the information you found in Step 3 about that particular resistance.

This is the EAM Transformation statement:

'I AM ready to transform/release this _____ (fill in the blank with what you found in Step 3). I release this from my energy, in all forms, on all levels, at all points in time.'

We repeat this statement three times to talk to the three powerful communicators and their associated functions or structures – your head, heart and hara. Remember to take a deep breath in and really breathe out, as the power of our Qi flowing into and out of the energy system also helps to create the shift.

The statement works by sending a command to all elements of our energy at once. Saying the words out loud releases the existing imprints, patterns and beliefs, and subconscious thinking, and it declares our intention. The words we use are specific to what we're doing in the energy field. We specify which resistance or reversal we're working on by describing what we found at Step 3.

Remember to Check You Are Clear

You'll notice that you feel empowered as you shift your vibrational frequency from what you found in Step 3 to what you released in Step 4. When you've done this, check your sway to make sure all resistance has gone. This gives us conscious confirmation of the release. You can do that by simply asking:

'Have I released all of this resistance about _____?'

You can also check by going back to what you experienced at Step 3.

- Energy – What does it feel like now in your body? Does it need a new description? Has it changed size, shape, location?
- Numbers – Reassess the number of thoughts, beliefs and patterns that you have. Use the sway to define the new number that may still be left.
- Emotions – Check with yourself and ask whether you still feel _____ emotion, or use the emotional scale to ask which emotions you have about that subject now.
- Clarifying Questions – Do you still have the resistance or reversal about _____?
- Visualization – Check in and see if the picture has changed.

If there is any remaining sensation, even if it's moved, changed or reduced, repeat Step 4 until your sway confirms you've released all of the resistance or reversal on that subject. Amend your Step 4 statement each time you repeat it to match the current experience. Be specific about what you're transforming in your energy – the more specific you are, the quicker your transformation.

If you complete Step 4 a couple of times and the resistance hasn't shifted, shrunk or moved, it's usually an energy reversal. Follow the steps with clarifying questions for that on page 158. **Always make sure you've released the resistance or reversed energy about that subject before you move on to Step 5.** Otherwise, you'll be trying to manifest while there's resistance, so you'd be pushing against it.

If you notice the sensation moving around your body, or have physiological pain after completing Step 4, this is perfectly normal. This includes headaches, backaches, toothache, nausea, dizziness or any other form of sensation. It's the resistance or reversed energy shifting from organs or other tissues, through the meridians and layers of your energy system and then out. If you still feel something in your energy field after a couple of minutes, it means you still have resistance to clear. Repeat Steps 1 to 4, and work on the sensation of the pain, for example, what size, shape, colour is it? Occasionally, the pain represents a new yet connected subject, which may require further clarifying questions to identify. Follow it through until you feel the pain has gone and confirm this by using your sway. Please do take care – if the pain is alarming and you're concerned, or have signs of a serious medical condition, please seek appropriate medical attention. Refrain from using EAM when there's a medical emergency. In such cases, please contact the relevant services.

It is common to cycle between Step 3 and Step 4 as you discover resistances and transform them. If you notice the emotions or sensations are very intense, it's a sign there is an energy reversal (see p. 158). You can complete Step 5 after each transformation or work on all the resistance you can identify around your subject and then do a really orgasmic Step 5.

You may complete Step 4 and notice that a new feeling appears, which feels positive. Check your sway and ask, '*Is this a feeling that I need to keep?*' If the answer is yes, use that to manifest on in Step 5. If not, it could be another resistance you need to transform, so repeat Step 4. Once you've completed this stage of the process, you're ready for Step 5.

Step 5 – Manifest

Step 5 is what EAM is all about. Allowing your light to shine, your energy field to open and expand, ready to receive, manifest and create what you want in life, and allowing all energy to be in flow, in all forms on all levels at all points in time. It's about bringing in the new paradigm, the higher vibration and love-based way of living. Remember the power of the observer – your conscious choice – powered by your words affects potential energy; you can literally command what you choose from nothingness into existence. To do this, we also use the power of those two words 'I AM'. It's like being your own genie. You'll feel the shifts from the first time you put this into practice, and it only continues to get better.

We command our energy and physical body in the same way we did with Step 4. Again, addressing the three energy centres – head, heart and hara – recalibrating your aura, meridians and chakras and free flow of Qi. This creates new imprints in our aura. Adding new thought forms, new emotions, patterns and messages which support us, creating a coherent state of flow.

Neurologically, this creates changes in the brain – as we engage our emotions we literally rewire the brain, creating new neural pathways. Because we do Step 5 in EAM, we transform the Qi that was previously stuck from Step 4 into something positive. You may also want to check with your sway that you're in alignment with the statement you're about to say at Step 5 by asking if you have resistance to receiving or asking for it.

People often get stuck at Step 5. They wonder which words to say or what to ask for, because you can ask for anything! It's up to you what you want to include – think of what you want to happen in relation to that subject. You can align to anything – a new belief, new feeling, greater flow of Qi, a new emotion, a new experience. Even world peace! Be expansive in your request. Remember you command the potential energy field. Everything is possible. Because it's ALL ENERGY. (Surely you've got the idea by now!)

To perform Step 5, we use a powerful statement in a similar way to Step 4. The best way to prepare yourself to do step 5 is first consciously open up your aura, chakras and funnel, and imagine light and colours flowing down and filling up your physical body. This helps to send out a powerful energetic message to the wider energy field – remember the universe responds to what you *feel* more than what you *think*, so engage all your senses. To do this use the same questions we used in Step 3 to assist creating your statement.

- What size/colour/shape is the feeling?
- Where is its location – inside/outside?
- Does it feel like another object, such as a heart or cloud?
- Is it hard/soft, still/moving/at speed?

Let that sensation and intention fill your body, imagine it going into each chakra, layer of your aura, to the cells, DNA and your energy field. Let it fill the room; imagine it flowing out from you into your home, your life, town, city and around the world. If you're unable to visualize, simply intend that is what you're doing. It will still work.

Then get into the right stance to best receive, stand with your arms in the air, above your head, connecting to the yang energy above you. Make sure your back is straight, head up sitting over your spine, so that source energy can flow through your system more easily. Have your feet hip-width apart so you ground the energy you receive into your body and draw energy up from the earth. Close your eyes to visualize what it is you want. See if you can create a picture in your mind's eye. Then finally, say the words out loud. This is the most powerful way to manifest. Always use 'I AM' instead of 'I'm' for your statement.

A powerful Step 5 stance

Then say the Step 5 Manifesting statement:

> **'I AM ready to allow/receive/feel_____ (fill in the blank with what you would like to think, feel or experience instead). I allow this into my energy, in all forms, on all levels, at all points in time.'**

Again, repeat this statement three times to speak to your head, heart and hara. You may want to repeat the group of three statements two or three times.

You may notice at Step 5 that you sway forward a lot! This is a good sign, as it means you're in alignment with your statements. Like a big YES from your energy. As you speak the words, they manifest into your future and almost pull you along the path. You may also notice your body bending, leaning backward or moving, tingling in your arms or legs and changes in posture. Allow these feelings in – this is the energy field realigning.

When composing your statement for Step 5, remember to use positive language. Instead of focusing on what you are avoiding. For example, instead of saying *'I AM ready to remain safe, protected and keep negative people away from me',* we want to manifest the positive, so focus on asking for what you do want to see, think, feel, do or experience: *'I AM ready to allow myself to be free and happy with everyone I spend time with.'*

As you progress with EAM, you'll see you can add in and adapt Step 5 statements. Make a note of your Step 5 statements, so you can align to those more in the future. The more you repeat them, the more true they'll become for you.

The Effects of Step 5

There are so many positive effects and benefits to Step 5, including:

- **Creating the new paradigm** – We create the new experience from a place of love and truth, creating a 'new world' within ourselves.
- **Commanding potential energy** – I AM commands the infinite field to become whatever you say following those words.

- **Increasing energy levels** – When you release, you go into a healing phase that can feel low in energy. Doing Step 5 brings your energy levels back up.
- **Reprogramming your energy field** – Remember your aura records everything you think, feel, say and do. Step 5 imprints new information so it becomes your new reality.
- **Strengthening your aura** – The receptive state and pose itself expands and strengthens your auric structure. Being in alignment naturally 'protects' you from other energies as your vibration is high and it's harder to be affected by other frequencies.
- **Sending positive energy into the field** – The high-vibrational intentions contribute to collective consciousness for other people to connect to.
- **Acting like an antenna** – The stance enables energy flow into your vibrational field. Your hands act like antennae as your meridians reach out from the ends of your fingers, extending into the different energy levels of your aura.
- **Empowering you to make a choice** – You are consciously choosing your path and making a clear declaration out loud about what you choose to think, feel or experience in your life.
- **Opening up your heart** – The stance also opens up and strengthens your heart, lungs, chest cavity, diaphragm and internal organs, which increases flow and receptivity in your whole body.
- **Rewiring the brain** – Our subconscious is always listening. By tuning into the emotion, becoming an energy match and simultaneously repeating the statement, we rewire neural pathways. This allows the brain to connect thought and emotion, and shape the experience to create a new set point.

- **Attracting what you want** – By feeling, imagining and consciously flowing light and energy to your new desire, you're a vibrational match and can attract anything you want.

How to Use Step 5

As well as using it to manifest good into your life, you can utilize Step 5 to bring changes in your vibrational frequency, thoughts and emotions. As you get used to it, you'll find your own ways to work with it – we want you to get creative. You can combine elements from the ideas below for powerful Step 5s. Here are a couple of ideas for statements.

1. Align Your Energy

There are lots of different ways to align your energy with Step 5. You can work on your general energy levels in simple ways with statements such as:

'I AM ready to allow myself to be 100% in flow. I allow this into my energy, in all forms, on all levels, at all points in time.'

'I AM ready to allow myself to flow freely through life. I allow this, etc ...'

'I AM ready to allow my chakras to be open and spin in the right direction. I allow this, etc ...'

'I AM ready to receive a flow of abundant energy. I allow this, etc ...'

2. Work on Thoughts and Beliefs

You can align to new beliefs, patterns or anything you want to associate with your mental awareness. Here are a few examples of statements you could use:

> *'I AM ready to allow myself to believe that I AM awesome. I AM more than good enough. I deserve everything I want to receive. I allow this, etc ...'*

> *'I AM ready to believe that life is meant to be good, it's meant to be fun, and I love everything about it. I allow this, etc ...'*

> *'I AM ready to allow myself to create a pattern of seeing the good in everything. I allow this, etc ...'*

3. Choose Your Emotions

Almost everything you want to experience is because you want to feel the emotion you'll have when you get it. You can align with any emotion you like. What does it feel like in your body?

> *'I AM ready to allow myself to receive love, freedom, peace and joy into my life. I allow this, etc ...'*

> *'I AM ready to allow myself to feel happy when I think about going to work. I allow this, etc ...'*

> *'I AM ready to allow myself to feel this warm glow of happiness in my solar plexus whenever I think about my life. I allow this, etc ...'*

4. Define New Experiences

You may want to create a new experience or attract something. To do that, change the way you get connected to the feeling of having it. Let it fill your energy. Then say:

'I AM ready to allow myself to connect to this feeling of happiness, empowerment, and excitement when I think about _____. I allow this, etc ...'

5. Change Relationships with People

This one we love – seeing the shifts in relationships as people understand how to change themselves and in turn see the change in others. An example of what that may look like is this:

'I AM ready to allow myself to be kind, thoughtful and loving toward _____ (name). I allow myself to feel love, peace and connection when in their company. I allow this, etc ...'

The Five Steps of EAM – A Quick Guide

Here's a simple quick reference guide for you to keep nearby when working through the Five Steps.

Step 1: Ask
This step is to give you clarity on what you need to shift. Ask your energy a simple question to see if it's something you need to work on. For example, *'Am I holding any resistance or worry when I think about making more money?'*

Step 2: Move
Your energy body will respond and give you the 'yes' or 'no' answer to the question you asked. Forward is usually 'yes' and backward usually 'no'. If you sway another way, check for energy reversals (see p. 158).

Step 3: Experience
This step is all about assessing what's happening in your energy when you think about that subject. You can perform this step in multiple ways. Choose which is appropriate for you.

1. What happens to your energy? Describe the size/colour/shape/location, etc.
2. How many of something do you have? Use the sway to identify the number.
3. Which emotions do you feel? Use the emotional scale.
4. Explore clarifying questions. Ask further questions to get more detail.
5. What do you see in your mind's eye? Describe the visual picture.

Step 4: Transform
Prepare and say your statement:

> *'I AM ready to release (whatever the subject). I release it from my energy in all forms, on all levels, and at all points in time.'*

Repeat this at least three times or until you can no longer feel the resistant energy. Remember to check it has released by asking your sway before moving to Step 5.

Step 5: Manifest
Prepare and say your statement:

> *'I AM ready to allow/receive/experience/think/feel (whatever the subject). I allow this into my energy in all forms, on all levels, at all points in time.'*

Repeat three times or more until you can feel that your energy is in alignment and you sway forward.

Powerful EAM Approaches

Now you understand the basics of the Five Steps of EAM, let's explore some powerful aspects of the process in more detail, beginning with how to deal with an energy reversal and then looking at some techniques and approaches that will help you work with it to best manifest your wonderful future.

How to Deal with an Energy Reversal

By now, you will probably have realized that you'll come across reversals frequently with EAM. Signs that you have an energy reversal to release include issues with your sway (see p. 129), getting 'stuck' at Step 4 with energy not being released, feeling intense emotions or becoming childlike (perhaps stamping your feet) when using EAM.

If you do find a reversal, you can help release the energy before or as you do EAM, by drinking water, going outside with bare feet or taking a shower to release. This often helps to clear it, along with EAM.

In Chapter 2, we saw they occur for a number of reasons – shock, trauma, events we had no strategy for, toxins in our environment, etc. When applying EAM, we may need to vary the steps when working on a reversal – for example, by asking additional questions at Step 3 to get conscious clarity on the reversal itself. This is because we needed to consciously 'understand the lesson' in order to let it release. We can also adapt the Step 4 or 5 statements.

Within EAM, we talk about reversals coming from many places, being passed down through generations in our family, preconception, conception, the womb or birth, this life and other lifetimes. In order to release fully, we need to be specific about the reversal we're releasing. We can do this through a series of questions that start fairly general before increasing in specificity.

When we suspect we have an energy reversal, begin by asking:

'Do I have an energy reversal?'
You may get an incorrect sway.

Next we need to know when it began, so you can ask:

- *Was it this life?*
- *Was it in the womb?*
- *Was it generational?*
- *Was it in a past life?*

Depending on the answer you can then ask your sway:

'How old was I when I created this reversal about _____?'
Sway up and down using the numbers process until you find the age you were.

'Which month of pregnancy _____?'
Use the sway to find which month.

'How many generations back in the family?'
Sway to see if it was 1, 2, 3 or more than 10 generations ago, for example.

'How many past lives ago?'
Sway to see if it was 1, 2, 3 or more than 10 lives ago, for example.

You can also ask exploratory questions to help build a picture or create a story. The reversal may be something you're aware of, through discussions with people or situations you know occurred at that age. If in the womb or other life, there'll be no conscious memory, so you may choose to ask:

This life:

- Who was involved ask their name or family member?
- Was It something they said/did/heard/believed?
- Where were you? e.g. home, school, work

You may suddenly remember something.

Pregnancy:

- Preconception (egg or sperm)
- Conception
- In the womb, how many months' pregnant?
- During labour or birth
- Was it something the mum said/did/felt/heard/believed?
- Who else was around or involved?
- If so, what was the belief/pattern/thought/energy about?

(Usually related to the subject of the reversal.)

Generational patterns:

- Which side of the family, mother/father?
- How many other people are influenced by it?
- Can you clear it for all of them?
- Are there any lessons to be learned?

Past life:

- Were you a woman/man/child?
- How old at the time?
- Did you/someone else get hurt/injured or die?
- Where you married/widowed?
- Rich/poor? Healthy/sick?

Use what you discover to formulate your Step 4 statement. You'll notice an addition to the Step 4 statement below to allow parts of your energy which may have split off at the time to come back to be fully integrated into your energy field again.

> *'I AM ready to release this energy reversal about _____ from age ___. I release anything that may prevent me from fully integrating all parts of me back. I release it from my energy in all forms, on all levels, at all points in time.'*

or

> *'I AM ready to release this energy reversal about _____ from ___ months in the womb, when _____ happened. I release anything that may prevent me from fully integrating all parts of me back. I release it, etc ...'*

or

> *'I AM ready to release this energy reversal about _____ from ___ generations back in my family on my _____ side. I release this for myself and _____ I release*

anything that may prevent me from fully integrating all parts of me back. I release it, etc ...'

or

'I AM ready to release this energy reversal from ___ past lives ago, when I was _____ aged ___ and _____ happened. I release any resistance that may prevent me from fully integrating all parts of me back. I release it, etc ...'

You'll need to repeat it two or three times or may need to ask additional questions for it to shift entirely. You may feel or sense the shift, and remember always check in with the sway with Step 4 to ensure it is released before you move to Step 5.

Ask the sway:

'Have I released this energy reversal about _____?'
If a reversal sticks or is unable to shift, you can ask:

'Is there something else I need to release or know?'
You may have to explore with some further questions.

You can also check:

'Has the part of my energy which separated come back?'
If it hasn't, you may need to do a Step 4 again.

If you've released it, which is confirmed by the sway, move onto Step 5.

Your Step 5 statement is in essence creative, so use it to reintegrate the parts of your energy, which may have split off at the time of the reversal. In your statement, be sure to include:

'I AM ready to allow myself to _____. I call all aligned parts of my energy back to me, so I may be complete. I allow this into my energy in all forms, on all levels, at all points in time.'

If you're still having challenges with the energy reversal and, having followed all of these steps, it's staying the same, this is where you may need additional support or further training to ask more relevant questions. See Resources and References at the back of the book. Sometimes you just also may need to sleep, rest, leave it for today; it's perfectly normal. We are like a giant puzzle: maybe another issue, which we are unaware of yet, has to release before it will fully go. You can still make progress. Just finish on a Step 5 or move onto another subject. Make a note and come back.

Working with Bubbles

When you have an issue that feels really big, or you're unsure where to start, there is a simple, clarifying technique to get everything out of your head and onto a sheet of paper. We call it the 'bubble method'. Even the act of writing itself is a powerful clarifying process. Let's use money as an example as it can be a very complicated issue to work through for some people.

On a piece of paper write MONEY in the middle and draw a circle. Then draw five other circles and connect them like balloons to the middle one. Make notes around the outside of each circle as suggested below – for each one you can use the suggested approaches to work through.

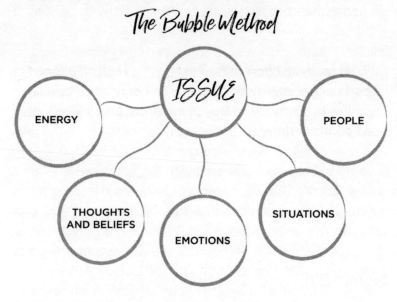

The Bubble Method

- In one circle, write the word ENERGY. Around the outside describe what this subject does to your energy; for example, heavy, drained, light, expanded. Use the energy approach (see p. 134) to discern this.
- In another circle, write THOUGHTS AND BELIEFS. Write down all the thoughts and beliefs or patterns you have about that subject. Use the numbers approach (see p. 136) to find how many of each you have.
- In another circle write EMOTIONS. You can use the emotional scale (see p. 97) or perhaps name the emotions you have about that topic. Write those down.
- In another circle write SITUATIONS. List any significant life events or memories connected to that subject or any you believe will be impacted by it in your future. Again, what happens to your energy, what thoughts or beliefs or emotions does it raise?

- In the last circle write PEOPLE. Write all the names of people involved, use EAM on how you feel about them, and what they have said or done.

Start by asking your sway which circle to work with first, and then which issue from around the circle to start with. Do Steps 1 to 4 of EAM, then ask the sway which to work on next. Continue to do this for a few of the issues. It's unlikely you'll need to work through everything, as the first few usually unweave the web. Keep adding notes as you work through. Ensure you finish on a powerful Step 5.

Use this process whenever you have a complex issue to approach, watch it unfold and fall away in your energy and your life.

Manifesting and Creating the Future

Manifesting is the act of consciously creating something. We all have the ability to manifest anything, yet it's a skill we're never taught. Your journey is about waking up this beautiful skill and putting it to good use.

When we think about manifesting, we usually think about a physical thing, such as a car, house or money. Yet the truth is that we manifest everything, even if we're doing so unconsciously. *Manifesting is the act of making something happen*. We are all natural manifestors. We can choose to manifest consciously by becoming aware of our energy, thoughts and emotions. Have you noticed your mind is constantly trying to get somewhere or achieve something? It's always dreaming something up, painting a picture or imagining something happening. You are manifesting all the time. Even when you sleep. So, make it your choice what you focus on.

When it comes to our energy system, it's the alignment of our head, heart and hara that creates the right environment to manifest vibrational frequency into physical form. Imagine a thought flowing down through your head, feeling the experience in your heart and receiving it in your hara to manifest physically. Similarly, your aura acts as a magnet, drawing in a thought on the mental level, then emotionally you begin to feel the love or excitement that's coming. Then you feel it in the etheric field, before it becomes a vibrational match to your physical body, when it can become a reality in your physical life.

Remember the more open and free-flowing energy you have in your funnel, chakras and layers of your aura, the quicker the manifestation. Your hara needs to be open, active and ready to receive.

When you're deliberately manifesting a situation or experience, remember to be very specific. It's best to write down exactly what you want, and to add in the words 'for the good of everyone concerned' when doing your Step 5. These words are important to ensure that however this happens it's a win–win for everyone. When manifesting, we never know how it will be delivered. Part of the journey is learning to surrender – the manifestation rarely happens how you imagined it, but always happens for your highest good.

The art of manifesting consciously is something you can develop. It happens through the focus, attention, energy and action you give to a particular situation. Most people are mis-manifesting their lives, because their focus is distracted, 'firefighting' what they perceive they want or focusing on what's missing. This becomes a vicious circle, creating more resistance and reversals, which then stand in the way of manifesting what we want and enforce the perception of what we want staying away.

We're often asked, *'How can I speed up getting what I want?'* The answer is simple: get in alignment and get intentional about it as quickly as possible. It's about you rather than time. It's about how ready your energy is to receive. It's about deliberately and systematically cleaning up your frequency, so that you can become a vibrational match to what you want. That is exactly what EAM allows you to do.

Five Steps to Successful Manifesting

With EAM, we talk about five key pieces of the puzzle that you need to have in place. Yes, you can create what you want without them in place, and I can guarantee every time something will go amiss when you miss a step. Your only job is to figure out *what* you want, then let go of *how* it will happen. Here are the five steps:

1. Create Your Vision

First you need some direction; your visualizations and intuitions will often be the inspiration for what to do.

2. Energy and Vitality

Then make sure your energy system is as receptive as possible. This means all of the energy structures and layers of your aura, including your physical body and vitality, are open and ready to receive what you want into your energy.

3. Thoughts and Words

Align your thoughts, beliefs and communication to support what you want.

4. Feelings and Emotions

Create positive emotions about that subject.

5. Aligned Action

Now it's time to take action, making aligned steps toward what you want. This will allow more magical opportunities, happy coincidences and the right people will fall into your path.

Be intentional with your manifesting, and be conscious of what you think, say and do. As you become purposeful with using EAM, watch your life change as you become more in flow with yourself and raise your alignment level. That is when the magic begins.

Finally, trust in the process. Often people believe having money is evil or manifesting material things is unspiritual. If everything is energy (which it is), does it matter in what form that energy arrives? We believe that all gifts are spiritual. Manifested knock-on-wood things are allowed! Maybe you're yet to manifest a car or a house, but be just as excited that you deliberately manifested a state of wellbeing. If you catch yourself judging the spirituality of someone else's manifestation, you can use EAM to work on those beliefs.

Overcome Common Side Effects

Everyone experiences shifts differently with EAM, because everything is energy; we never know how it might manifest. You know yourself best, so please take responsibility for yourself. EAM is a very powerful process.

In all the years and thousands of people we have worked with, only one client was concerning, when she experienced the side effects of a healing cycle. As we worked through it with EAM, it led to a huge healing experience for her. She uncovered and released trauma and memories of sexual abuse that had been hidden from her subconscious. This became a huge part of her journey and she is now an EAM mentor, teaching people how to use EAM to powerfully connect with their sexuality.

Stress and Healing

As you work on releasing resistance you'll naturally go into a healing phase. If your body has been in stress/resistance or you've felt overwhelmed for some time, your body will go through a healing process to rejuvenate and get well. This often looks like low energy, tiredness, headaches, exhaustion, sleep disruption or vivid dreams, general aches, the flu, a cold or a build-up of mucus, and yucky things leaving your body – poo, wee, burping, tooting or anything else you'd rather keep to yourself. It's all a sign of release and that your body is in the healing phase.

Many other practices tell you to 'sit with these emotions'. This is because other processes are waiting for the subconscious to 'bubble up' the issue to get clarity. With EAM you have the sway, which means you can explore using the Five Steps and move your way through the healing phase much quicker.

There's often a spike in the journey where you're 'tested' on that subject, and it may feel as though it has 'come back'. Use EAM to work through the healing phase. When you 'emerge' from the other side you'll be more aligned, coherent and experience a new level of life.

I Keep On Crying!

Tears mean you're releasing the resistance, which is better than holding it in. If you end up in a shower of tears, use the Five Steps of EAM. If you can, then use the sway to discover what the resistance is about. If you're deep in the emotion and unable to find words, focus on the feeling. Use the 'what's happening in your energy' steps of EAM (see p. 134) to release it. Or shorten it to, *'I AM ready to release these tears/sadness from my energy. I release it in all forms, etc ...'* Repeat this statement until you feel the emotion subside. Then explore it with the sway.

It May Get Worse Before It Gets Better
When using healing modalities like EAM, what you work on may seem to get worse before it gets better. While energy cannot be destroyed – it moves like a wave, for example – the resistance is held in your energy field. As it transforms, it sends a tsunami of pent-up Qi through the different layers of your aura out into your life experience before the tide returns and brings back what you've been asking for. For instance, having arguments with your partner when you've been working on relationships will then resolve and you find a deeper connection. Or you may lose money when you've been working on having more, only to get more from another source. Stay with it and know that change is on the way.

Positive Side Effects
Aside from the short list of possible negative side effects, we've talked about all of the benefits of being in alignment and what it can do for you. We wanted to share a few of the other amazing benefits that can happen as a result of using EAM.

- Change in posture, feel lighter and taller as you're no longer held down, having released the heaviness, your aura can expand.
- No longer overreact, easily become upset or emotional. You're calmer, more open and softer toward others.
- Thoughts are more positive; memories no longer hold an emotional charge or are forgotten.
- Attract more opportunities and positive 'coincidences' because you're more connected to your intuition.
- Able to access new information and have inspired ideas.
- 'Magical' shifts in people's response and interactions with you.

- Rapid life changes because you're free, empowered and take more action.
- Look younger, brighter skin, wrinkles disappear, eyes sparkle, inner glow, lose weight.
- Changes in physical health conditions even the body begins to repair, organs return to health.
- More positive and empowered knowing everything is working for you.
- Develop your intuition and receive more 'messages'.
- Charisma, magnetism and presence will increase.

In Summary

Wow, what a journey! Now you *really* know how to use EAM. These are the basics, but certainly more than enough to get you started and change so many areas of your life. You've explored the sway, why we use it and how it creates this powerful connection. You've learned the Five Steps of EAM, how to adapt them to work for any situation and what makes EAM different. Now you can put it into practice every day. It's time to get ready to change your life and create the life you deserve.

PART THREE

HOW TO CHANGE
YOUR LIFE WITH EAM

Chapter 7

BEGINNING THE JOURNEY

Now you understand your energy from the scientific and spiritual aspects, and you know the Five Steps of EAM, you have a solid foundation to put it all into practice. It's time to get real – this is what we're here for, to begin changing your life.

EAM is more than a tool, it's a way of life. Everything is energy, which means EAM can be applied to any situation. This can be both empowering and overwhelming. Where do you begin? What comes first? What's REALLY possible? In this part of the book, we'll begin exploring the practicalities of using EAM. We'll share the step-by-step way to put this into practice for yourself.

We'll start by exploring some of the myths around the personal development industry and learning a few consciousness shifts you need to make in order to discover how to live life in the new paradigm and bring EAM to change every area of your life. So, get ready to release the beliefs, patterns and stories that hold you back and create a new attractive vision for your amazing future.

Before we begin, you really need to hear this. **There is never a right time to change your life!** No one else will change it for you. You have to do it. So, please stop putting it off! We're here with you. **Now is the time.**

Dispelling Myths

There are a few self-help myths that we often come across where people have read, seen or interpreted information or half-stories. These same myths can hinder our journey to changing our life, so we want to clear them up right now.

1. To Change Your Life, Just Think Positively and Say Your Affirmations

The truth is that you *have to* let go of resistance or negativity first. You have to let go of any resistant energy, thoughts, beliefs or emotions *before* you do the positive thinking and affirmations, otherwise your energy field will contradict the words you use. Yes, affirmations, positivity and focus are important, but you need to transform (Step 4) the resistance before you can manifest (Step 5).

2. The Law of Attraction Is Quick and Always Gives Instant Results

This myth has led to a world of people looking for a 'quick fix' solution to changing their life. When their manifestation hasn't arrived in 24 hours, they give up on themselves, thinking they're wrong or broken. They then change their focus and give attention to it *not* being there, which creates the same.

We've seen people release issues with EAM, which would take years or months with other therapies, in minutes. When they're gone, your ability to attract can be fast; however, sometimes manifestations are meant to take time. It's the point between asking and receiving where you have to learn trust and surrender. Maybe other pieces of the puzzle have to fall into place, timing has to be right, or you need to be ready to receive all you're asking for.

3. It's All About an Abundant Mindset

No, being in alignment and changing your life is about more than your mindset. That is only one expression of your life. You must understand *all* the key elements of the manifesting/change your life/personal development puzzle. We've heard people say, *'Just write your gratitude journal'*, or *'Just meditate'*, or *'Just think positively'*. Then it doesn't work and no one tells you why.

These practices are tools to enable you to harness your energy and they work brilliantly when you are in flow. Yet, they only form part of the picture. Everything is energy, and energy can only be in one of three states. When you apply EAM first, it works wonderfully alongside these tools too.

4. Just Ask and You'll Receive

The Law of Attraction is seen as a magical principle that will make you a millionaire without you having to do anything. This links back to that 'quick fix' mentality. However, the Law of Attraction is an active rather than passive process. You have to get involved in it to make it manifest. It's more than something to focus on when you want to manifest: it's a way of life.

What determines the answer you receive is really the vibrational question you ask. But what you attract is rarely in the form you expect. The guidance you receive is often more subtle. It may be a chance meeting, an intuitive nudge, finding a book, meeting a person or hearing from a friend. People believe manifesting only means receiving the thing they asked for. In truth, we're manifesting and receiving all the time. We do get an answer; we just often miss the message. You have to take action, otherwise you'll never find the answer you've been asking for.

5. You Have to 'Dig' for the Root of Your Unhappiness Or Talk It Out

Many other self-help methods or traditional forms of therapy require you to relive the past. For some people, it's helpful. For some it's painful. By re-energizing past experiences, we put ourselves back into the energetic state we were in at the time. With EAM, you can release and transform anything in your biofield without 'digging', 'finding the root' or 'talking it out'. You can get clarity on things without the pain. By releasing the energy of the situation, you also create change across multiple levels of your experience at all once.

A Shift in Consciousness

Moving from the old paradigm to the new is simply a shift in conscious awareness of what you think, say and do, and how you behave. The old paradigm comes from resistance or reversals, which will prevent us making changes. The new paradigm is about being in alignment. This is exactly what EAM facilitates; it releases the old (Step 4) and allows in the new (Step 5).

Here are a few examples of a paradigm shift:

- From letting fear hold you back to sharing love and creating freedom of choice.
- From believing in lack to being in abundance and seeing we have more than enough.
- From controlling others using blame, shame and manipulation to self-responsibility and personal empowerment.
- From self-worth based on what you 'have' to inner self-esteem – being conscious of who you are.

- From feeling affected by your external world, to knowing that you affect the world.
- From 'reacting' to situations outside of you to being consciously creative.
- From believing everything is wrong to knowing everything is alright.
- From using blame, shame, fault and guilt without accepting responsibility, to recognizing our responsibility for what's happening.
- From not good enough to being more than enough.

As you go on this journey, you'll see that the old paradigm falls away and the life you want begins to emerge. The new paradigm becomes your new normal. Every time you do EAM, you're changing the paradigm for you and the wider world. Let's take a closer look.

Simple Principles

Here is a helpful checklist of some simple principles that support living in the new paradigm:

- **Pay attention in the moment** – Notice your energy throughout the day. Readjust and align, the more in flow you are, the more will come, at a faster speed.
- **Notice goosebumps** – This is a sign that you're in truth, alignment or manifesting your dream, vision or pathway.
- **Everything is energy** – When we truly live this, the fear drops away because you know you've got the power to change it.
- **Take responsibility** – Own what you think, feel, do and how you communicate. It's all down to you and no one else.

- **Release the fear** – Any overwhelm, stress or anxiety you experience is a sign you need to do some EAM to bring clarity.
- **Make alignment your top priority** – Get yourself in alignment before you do anything.
- **Step out of the drama and into your power** – Choose where and how you spend time and energy.
- **Find forgiveness** – The only person affected by unforgiveness is you. Do EAM and let it go.
- **Be compassionate** – Everyone is on a journey. Understand others without having to jump into the drama with them.
- **Recognize your greatness** – See how powerful you already are.
- **Have high hopes for the future** – Release fear of what 'may' happen, otherwise you're creating what you don't want.
- **Let go of time** – You don't run the schedule. Trust the universe to deliver what you want when you're energetically ready.

Let go and allow the universe to guide you.

- **Sit still and allow** – Sit and connect to the flow of abundance at least once a day, to open your energy system to receiving, then go and take inspired action.
- **Shift your attention away from lack** – See the abundance in *everything*. Whether it's money, time, love, people or clients, what you focus on sends a message to the universe.

- **Be generous with everything** – Give from a place of alignment knowing there's always more to come.
- **Release the 'needing'** – This keeps what you want away. Release resistance, be open to receiving and trust that it's coming.

Setting Intentions

One of the most common ways we attempt to change our life is to set a goal or intention. We go into our head, overthink, use logic and take action to make something happen.

Ironically, this drive and push is often why people are unable to achieve their goal as it creates resistance. If you have to 'push', it means you're pushing against something else, usually yourself and a greater source of life.

Mostly, we've set the intention from a place of lack or fear, believing happiness will come when we have it. If you apply this energy of 'push', it manifests more unwelcome energy. You'll be unable to lose weight, give up smoking or drinking or earn more money because you've created resistance. The easy EAM way is to create from a place of joy, passion or belief. Align your energy, thoughts and emotions and watch it manifest into your life.

Releasing the Past

So many people define themselves and their lives by what happened in their past, as if it somehow explains or defines their future. We've all had life experiences that shaped us. Think about this for a second. *Before* it happened, did we use it to define ourselves? No, how could we? What changed? Simply a shift in our frequency, perspective and the story we held onto.

What will happen when you release *that* story, letting go of the beliefs and emotions from it that you use to define you? Whether it's you or someone else who did something, you have to clean it up and release the energy connected to the old stories, so you can move forward. Only then can you create a new narrative.

You may ask what to do when someone has 'done' something to you? Like, *really* hurt you, physically, emotionally or mentally? How do you find it in yourself to do the energy work when the pain inside you is so deep? Some of us have been in situations or relationships where we've experienced abuse or traumatic situations. Those will undoubtedly create resistances or reversals that are stuck in our energy field. You may feel angry, fearful, depressed or alone. It may feel as if no one understands you or your pain. We get it. Believe us, we really do.

We meet a lot of people who've been in situations like rape, attack or abuse, and they say, '*I don't understand how I attracted that*', or '*The Law of Attraction doesn't work.*' No one consciously invites an attack. These situations can, however, be 'attracted' on a subconscious level, below our conscious awareness. We attract what's in our energy, even if we're unaware of it. Maybe we feel unworthy, useless or alone, or even attacked in some way? It could be a pattern from a past life, or passed on through the family lines. Resistances come from many places.

This categorically does *not* place the blame on you. We're unable to control other people in our life. If something does happen, whatever the reason, the only thing we can ever be responsible for is *our response* to it. When something traumatic happens, we have two choices. We can let it define us for the rest of our lives, or we let it go and become all the stronger for it. We're sure you can guess which one we'll suggest.

Remember, we may have issues to resolve too. What wrongs in your life do you need to put right? Where have you done something that you know affects you or has hurt others? What if you could clean it up? What apologies do you need to make? What resistance do you need to release first? These imprints are held in your auric field – the guilt, remorse, self-hatred, protection and walls. There will be an energy entanglement between you and them because of it, even if they're no longer a part of your life or passed on. Even if that person is no longer in your life, you can still do the energy work and release it from your field.

How to Let Go

What happened to us was a set of circumstances, which will have impacted our energy. Now if we *really* believe that everything is energy (which it is), we can choose right now to *change our experience of what happened*. This is one of the most powerful practices of EAM. It's a phenomenal way to change our experience of trauma or hurt on many levels. Depending on how far down the quantum physics rabbit hole you want to go, by doing the energy work you can actually change that experience throughout time, for you and everyone else involved.

We can get stuck holding on because letting go can feel like letting them or ourselves off the hook. The truth is, the person you're letting off the hook is *you*. The aim is to be in alignment toward this person. Imagine releasing the trapped energy, recurring thoughts and memories, heavy emotions, resistances and reversals from that situation. You can use EAM to literally change your experience of it. You have the power and the tools to heal the impact it has had.

If you've experienced trauma or been affected by what someone else has done to you, or what you may have done to others, please know your path is your own. You have two choices: you can either let it hold you or take back your power by reclaiming yourself energetically, emotionally, mentally and spiritually. Your life is far from over; you have so much more to live. So, live it. You can start today. No matter what has happened in your past, you still have your future. Using EAM you can claim it back for yourself.

Exercise –
What Happened in Your Past?

Imagine you're meeting us for the first time. We've shared a bottle of wine and you're in full-on story mode, giving the unedited version of your life. Write the answers to these questions in your journal:

- What's the story you would tell us about you?
- Who else is involved?
- What did they say and do?
- What did you say and do?
- What did you believe and feel about the situation, them and yourself?
- Who was to blame?
- What did it stop you or allow you to do?
- How has it affected your energy, thoughts or emotions?
- How does it make you feel when you think about your past?
- How has it affected you and your life since then?
- What, if any, apologies do you need to make?
- What resistance do you need to release first?

- If you could go back and wave a magic wand, what would you do differently?
- Anything else you feel you need to get off your chest?

Now, using EAM, look at what happens to your energy when you think about your answers. What are the thoughts and beliefs you see in there? What emotions do you feel? Use some of the approaches we talked about in EAM Step 3 (see p. 133) to help you define issues to address with Step 4. Then align yourself to a new story – what you want to happen now – and allow that to be your Step 5.

Staying the Course

When we begin a transformational journey, we think the change will happen in an instant. Truthfully, there'll be days when you want to give up, and wonder if you've changed at all. Friends and loved ones who are no longer a match to you energetically leave your life. There'll be days when you're on top of the world, and you'll want to shout from the rooftops how awesome life is. You'll meet new people, create new synergies, it will feel like electric goosebumps. Life will grow, develop and manifest faster than you ever imagined. Stick with EAM and, over time, you'll develop a more consistent pattern of being in alignment, to benefit you and others around you.

We've all been led to believe that everything is instant. If we haven't achieved something straight away, we give up or try the next 'fad' promising a quick answer. While EAM is quick and the energetic transformations can be fast for one issue, the truth is that changing your life is far from a quick process. It's about the cumulative effects of changing your vibrational frequency, the way you think, communicate and act, every day.

We've taken a look at the past; now let's see where you are, what may be holding you back, and what you need to change to move past this point and allow the future that you want to become your present experience. Do you have situations or people in your life that drain your energy? You have to change that, otherwise you'll never have enough time or energy to get on with what's important to you.

We have to make space. Let go of the old to allow in the new.

Look at your life right now. What's going really well, or not? What makes you happy or sad? What areas of your life, or people, do you avoid? What topics have you buried away? What could be better or changed? These are such important questions to address because they all create resistance in your vibration, on every subject. It's all energy, as we know.

How often do we look at our life and wonder how it could be 'better'? Do you already have a really long list of what you want to change? To change our lives, we have to close the imaginary gap between where we *think* we are and where we *think* we want to be. Before now, this reality of where you think you want to be may have been eluding you. That's because the journey to change your life and close the gap is an *energetic one*. Which is never solved with thinking.

The big question to ask is: *'Is this REALLY what I want?'* Do you know for sure the future you want is really yours? Or is it a construct of what you *think* you want? Is it *your* dream, or what society, family, or friends have said is right, or led you to believe will make you happy? Is it possible that you've taken on a plan to change your life that may belong to someone else?

We often push and struggle to create a life that we think will make us happy, only to wake up and realize it's miles away from what we really want. We also think that we have to 'get somewhere' in order to change our lives. We put ourselves on this endless journey to an unknown destination changing circumstances outside of us – relationships, work, money, car, house – believing that this is what needs changing, when it's always an inner game. If you know the future you're creating belongs to someone else instead of you, please stop. To change your life, you have to want it with every inch of your soul, otherwise how will you remain committed enough to create it? It also means you're out of alignment with it, too, so it will never come to you. This is ultimately good if you are manifesting someone else's dream, yet it's a bad thing if you keep giving energy to it.

Your Attractive Vision

This is about you knowing where you want to go. I was first introduced to the power of vision by a wonderful friend, Tamsen Garrie, author of *The Act of Attraction in Business*. In it she describes vision in the following way: *'A vision is a mental image produced by the imagination, and it's usually a long-term view of the future. Many people have a vision; however, not all visions are effective when we talk about Attraction. It's about creating an attractive vision.'*

The source of your vision is from your subconscious by tapping into your energy field. It's a wonderful expansion, way beyond what you think or believe is possible. We're tapping into that bigger all-knowing source of potential energy, which transcends our experience of time and space. When you connect to your attractive vision, it's often far bigger than you could ever imagine.

When you know your vision, you know what thoughts and beliefs you need, what actions to take, what living life that way will feel like. Your vision is your guide to changing your life; use it to create your step-by-step plan. It assists you in making decisions too. If something you're doing in your life doesn't match your vision, you need to find a way to change it. The reason we want to attract things in our life is because of the sense of peace, love, freedom or joy we think it will bring us. The irony is that to bring them into our life we have to already have those feelings.

To bring your vision to life is to let go of thinking about it being *someday* and make it *today*. We know what you see around you today may be different from your vision; what you can change today is your frequency to make it match the life you want. You can live with the sense of freedom and find a way to live it now. To connect to your vision, you need to allow yourself to get into a meditative state. By doing so we bypass the limitations of our conscious awareness.

When we work with our clients, we lead them through powerful visualization exercises to step into the future version of themselves, and we tap into a life that is even bigger than anything they ever dreamed possible. The more you use EAM to release resistance in your energy, the clearer your own vision becomes. Over the months and years that you use this process, you'll notice your visions and intuition become clearer.

To create your new future, you want to get into a meditative state and take yourself on a journey to a point in your future where everything is as you want it to be. EAM will help guide you through how your energy feels, what positive thoughts, beliefs and emotions you experience. What are your health, home and relationships like? How do you enjoy life? What's your financial situation? What do you do for a living or your passion, and how do you impact the world with what you do?

The first time you do connect to your vision it's common to see nothing. You may only have a sensation of something. Perhaps you'll see only colours or a few words. That's okay, keep working with it.

Your vision is constantly evolving, and everyone should revisit their vision at least once a month (ideally daily). The more you align and expand your vibration, the more pieces of the puzzle become clear. Once you know pieces of your vision, speak it out loud as often as possible. Our words have power, and the more you speak of it, the quicker it comes into your reality. When people ask what you do, share your vision. Talk about what you're creating. This makes magic happen. The right people, places and opportunities will be presented to you. This is how you manifest because people are inspired by the future of what's possible.

Creating a New Story

Very often, what stops us from changing our lives is that we create resistance. We unknowingly put obstacles in our way all the time. You may call them excuses, stories, patterns or fear. Whatever way they're showing up for you, it's usually self-inflicted resistance and reversals. Ouch! We know that's hard to hear. We can say that because we've been there so many times ourselves. If you only knew how many times our 'stories' got in the way. Is that stuff really true or is it something we could choose to let go? We can change our life, by creating a new narrative, by stepping into a new paradigm.

You have the power to write a new story.

These patterns can be expressed in 101 ways. It could be self-harming or sabotaging patterns of putting yourself last, keeping yourself busy, being too stressed, having poor boundaries, lack of commitment, procrastination, comparing ourselves to others, focusing on materialistic outcomes, never asking for support, patterns of anger or any repeating emotion, feeling helpless, overwhelmed, powerless, allowing people to treat you badly, giving others control of your life, getting in debt, ignoring or pushing away love … The list goes on and on and on.

We're going to invite you, right now, to let those patterns, stories and beliefs go, because the cost to you to keep holding onto them is way too high. This is your life at stake here and it's up to you to do this. We hold onto these stories because they keep us 'safe' and give us a reason to keep our lives as they are. We can let go of responsibility, stay in our comfort zone, and maintain the status quo. Remember, one of our brain's primary needs is to feel safe so anything that makes us feel unsafe will result in fear, which is resistance or reversal. We know how to deal with those.

When you work through these stories, patterns, beliefs or emotions with EAM, the way you think and feel is never the same. So, how can they be true if what you feel about them changes? Does that tell you that it's all just energy?

Do you see how all of these experiences, whether they're something you recognize or something you're unaware of, can hold you back and prevent you from attracting and creating into the life you really want. While we hold them in our energy we're more likely to attract more of the same!

So, we've taken a look at the past, we have some clarity on where we are, and have taken a brief look at the future – now it's time to close the energy gap between where we are and where we want to be. We're going to take time to look at your soul, your life and your work – these are the next steps to evolving you and your energy and ultimately changing your entire life. Are you ready to write the next page?

Chapter 8

THE 10 ELEMENTS
OF THE ENERGY EVOLUTION

We're now going to explore the 10 elements of the Energy Evolution – the step-by-step journey to changing your life using EAM across three key life areas: your **soul**, your **life** and your **work**. Each of the 10 elements includes a practical exercise to support you on your way. It's time to take what we've learned about EAM and put it into practice!

This journey begins with your soul, the pieces of your life that you can never share with anyone: your spiritual connection, thoughts and beliefs, emotions and physical health. We then move on to your life – your environment, relationships and lifestyle. Finally, we look at your work, so we can live abundantly and make money, follow our passion and purpose and make an impact.

The Energy Evolution

Most people who want to make lasting changes in their life approach it in a haphazard way, without a system, process or structure. Attempting to solve the right problems in the wrong order. When it goes wrong they feel like a failure. With EAM, you align your energy and systematically work your way through each area of your life. Step-by-step, you allow yourself to create more flow and momentum. This is how we create true and lasting change.

We often get so focused on our biggest challenge and unsuccessfully attempt to wrestle it to the ground. We often think, *'If I can solve this ONE thing, then my life will be sorted.'* That might be a relationship, money, career, business or your health. When we identify 'one thing' it's just a tiny piece of the puzzle. You're *more than* one thing. Your life is more than one thing. You're a beautiful, complex, multifaceted being, living life on many levels all at once. There is no *one thing* about you. On the flip side, if you attempt to change your whole life all at once it will be overwhelming. So, how do you know where to start?

To answer this overarching question, we created the Energy Evolution, a step-by-step journey to changing your life with EAM. It's a simple, systematic way that works with the structure of your energy field, approaching one subject in your life at a time. It creates a domino effect, which multiplies the energy. As you unstick each consecutive area, the momentum of energy begins to change your life more rapidly for you. You feel more empowered as everything begins to feel easier. With the Energy Evolution programme we look at your life in three main areas: your soul, your life and your work.

Your **soul** is a collection of four elements of your life that only you ever experience. These are your spiritual or energetic makeup, your thoughts and beliefs, your emotions and physical health. These are areas you're unable to share with anyone. They're the elements that make you, you.

Your SOUL is the part that makes you, you!

Then there are areas of your **life** that you share with people close to you; what you live life for. They're your home or physical environment, your relationships, connection to others, and your lifestyle – what makes up your life outside of work.

When we talk about your **work**, it means how you express your soul's life work in the world to create money, live abundantly, connect with your passion, discover your purpose and make your impact in the world.

By working this way, and by bringing all the areas of your soul, life and work into alignment first, you'll then have the focus, stability, power and capacity to make a real difference to others.

There's so much more to the Energy Evolution than we can squeeze into the pages of this book. Here, we will take a high-level view and introduce you to a handful of the hundreds of step-by-step exercises available to work through your life with EAM.

We begin with your soul, systematically working our way through the three outer layers, then onto mental, emotional and physical layers. As we release the low vibrational imprints (resistances and reversals) in each level, our energy expands and becomes stronger. This makes it easier for the resistance from the other levels to transform more easily.

In Chapter 4, we talked about our hara and physical bodies needing to be open and in alignment in order to manifest more easily. We also need our physical body to be healthy and in a state of coherence. If your body is sick, it means you are unable to vibrate at a higher level, and your progress may be slower. This is also why we work on the outer layers of your aura first. By systematically clearing, we reduce stress and pressure in the energy field, which is creating signals sent into the body via the nervous system, which cause the physical symptoms. This puts our physical body in a better place to heal, increase vitality and realign to optimal health, so it is better able to transform.

Once your physical energy is healthy, including your physical environment, relationships and lifestyle, you'll be able to live a more expansive, meaningful and connected life. And once these foundations are in place – we have our energy system and life elements in alignment – we have a greater impact with our soul's work. Ultimately, there is no 'one thing' that will change your life. It's a systematic, cumulative effect that will create the biggest shifts, which is why we work this way within EAM.

Element 1 – Energy Connection

Our understanding of our inner and outer worlds is constantly expanding. We once believed that the world was flat, before we knew about the giant interconnected universe. Our connection to energy and our understanding of it is also evolving. Yet, right now, know that you are the key. You're the power behind what's happening.

Let's take a look at the first element, your soul – your spiritual or universal connection with your energy. This relates to the outer layers of your aura: the astral, celestial and divine. Our intention is to align our energy system, like rewiring or plumbing to ensure the 'machine' is in a receptive state. We're cleaning up the energy field, imprints, past experiences. We need to ensure the system is working well with us to begin with. This prevents anything energetically hindering you as you go on this journey to change your life.

This energy influences more than our perception of the world, our thoughts and feelings, and our physical body;

it affects *everything* we come into contact with. Have you ever walked into a room when someone has been told some wonderful news? The air is electric, you can feel the happiness! Likewise, you've certainly been in a closed space with someone who is in a bad mood and can feel their vibe like a heavy weight. Our energy is always influencing other people. Before you shake hands with someone your energies have already met – you're literally standing in the soup of someone else's beliefs, thoughts and feelings!

Your energy affects everything in your world – relationships, your communication with others, what you say, *how* you say it, even what you're thinking. People don't have to be psychic to pick up on what we're vibrating about them; they can sense it through energy.

One super simple way to use EAM to keep yourself in flow is to check if your head, heart and hara are in alignment. Ask the sway individually if each one is in flow, then you can use the Five Steps to align yourself to bring them back into sync. This is a simple way to keep your energy system working.

Similarly, you can align your energy field by checking in with all the layers of your aura or each of your chakras. Are they open and free-flowing? Stay in alignment by checking in regularly and make this part of your morning routine. Again, you can use the sway to check what's happening with each level of your aura or chakras. Use the Five Steps to keep them open and aligned. For example, ask your sway, '*Is the emotional layer of my aura open?*', or '*Is my base chakra open?*' If 'yes', move to the next one, if 'no', do the Five Steps. You can quickly whip through them while brushing your teeth. By doing this you make sure your energy is open, your structures are strong, and your aura is intact.

Other subjects to consider in this first element of the Energy Evolution would be your relationship with time. Work through systematically, cleaning up your past and future timelines. You can look at conception, time in the womb and birth, working through your childhood, patterns passed down through the generations, and so much more. All of these make up the key elements that define our current life experience.

Element 1 Exercise – Am I Pushing?

Throughout this book, we explore all the areas where you can use EAM to align the key aspects of your life. That said, alignment is more than a task on your 'to do' list, to be ticked off when done. It's something to do in each moment, each day. We want you to become so tuned into how you feel that nothing takes you away from that. So, whenever you feel like you're pushing, unsure or feel low vibration, it's a sign of resistance, which means time to do some EAM.

Here are a few examples of questions you can use at Step 1: Ask. Once you get your answers, follow the rest of the Five Steps of EAM to release any resistance and get yourself even more in alignment.

- Am I feeling resistance about _____?
- Is there resistance in my energy when I think about _____?
- Am I pushing to make _____ happen?
- Am I working against the flow about _____ to make it happen?
- Is now the right time for me to be doing _____?

- Do I have resistant thoughts/feelings/beliefs about _____ which prevent me from getting on with it?

Get used to asking these questions all day, every day. This is all part of noticing how you feel and how in or out of alignment you are in each moment. Remember, instead of the push, we need to take aligned action – it wins every time against the push because it engages your hara, which is following your heart and is guided by your head. If you're in resistance and try to take action, you'll never create the life you desire or are aligned to; you'll create more of the same chaos and confusion. Alignment of your whole energy system allows a flood of inspired ideas, insights, thoughts and actions to come to you. These are the seeds of manifesting.

Element 2 – Create an Abundant Mindset

In this element, we continue our journey into the energy field. Here, we explore the mental level of our aura. We will take a brief look at thoughts, beliefs and self-sabotage patterns. Beyond this, as you journey further into the Energy Evolution, you'll understand more about changing your set points, core values and beliefs, generational patterns, personality traits and language, releasing self-imposed limitations. Ultimately, our intention is to quiet the internal chatter, gain clarity and insight, and develop a mindset to support our journey.

We once believed it was our brain that we needed to 'control', that once we could tame this beast everything else would be fine. We now know that to change our beliefs we also need to address our energy. In fact, our beliefs are an expression of frequency. Let's see how we can get the mental level of our energy to support us.

This is about aligning those 'hidden' pieces that make us, well, US! You'll recognize this as our cognitive thoughts and experience of reality. Many of the beliefs, thoughts and patterns that create our mindset come from a place of protection or fear. Using EAM, we want to bring to light those unknown parts of our consciousness, integrating them with our cognitive thoughts in a way that serves us now.

The good news is that our life is probably very different to how we *think* it is. The flip side of this means we're living the life our 'mind' has constructed. We know that the mental level of our auric field is made of our thoughts, beliefs, memories, patterns and experiences. They cloud our ability to be objective, therefore shaping our reality. Our aim with EAM is to change our interpretation of experiences to ones that are supportive.

Understanding Our Thoughts

From a spiritual or energetic perspective, our thoughts are forms of fast-moving, higher-vibrational energy, which we're unable to see with the naked eye, yet we experience them in every moment. Energetically, we know our thoughts are stored in the mental level of our aura. Remember, we said our aura is a recording device? Well, our thoughts are often replayed over the soundtrack from those records. While you may be having a new experience, there is always this background noise and filtering from our past.

On our journey of development, we want our thoughts to be ones that support us, cheering us on. If we're holding a lifetime of resistant beliefs, they're literally going to be weighing down our vibrant life force, preventing new information coming in, and sending out mixed messages through our aura. This is part of the reason we mis-manifest, because those beliefs are still in our energy.

From a psychology perspective, resistant thoughts keep us stuck in circles, diverting our energy and attention, and preventing us from being focused in the moment. Over time, you'll become the conscious creator of your thoughts rather than let yourself be at their mercy.

Managing Our Memories

Our memories are a type of thought, our interpretation of past situations, distilled and distorted through our filters. The big question is always: are our memories real? Have you ever noticed how over time a memory can seem to change? Maybe the next time you tell someone the story it's changed ever so slightly; maybe there's a little bend of the truth or an elaboration of a certain fact. If you continue to tell the slightly altered story for long enough it becomes a 'truth'. Did it really happen that way? Or is this how *you* recall it.

We need to decide if our memories serve us. We naturally refer to the past in order to assess our present (and our future). If the memories we hold are untrue, we could be shaping our whole life on shaky ground.

Changing your memories has an amazing ripple effect. When you no longer have resistance, you make new choices, take new steps and find new ways of behaving. This begins to change your life and the life of others around you.

Yvette's Experience

When I was about 4 or 5, I was playing at a friend's house and fell into the swimming pool, underneath the pool cover. I wasn't a very good swimmer. I remember having to fight my way up to the surface under the cover, gasping for air, swallowing water and trying to breathe. I grew up avoiding swimming because I always felt like I was drowning.

I've since worked on those memories so that I AM now much more confident in the water and I love it, especially when taking my son swimming. Making the time to do this work on myself means I am able to be in the water and teach him a very important skill – learning how to swim. Had I allowed that fear to affect me and what I did, what would that have created? Another child who is afraid of, and who is unsafe near, water. You have the power to change stories too.

Changing Our Patterns

A pattern is still a thought, with a lot of momentum, which creates a habitual way of thinking or behaving so it becomes easy to do. Patterns can be learned, inherited or passed down. We often aren't even aware patterns are there, because it's 'normal' – it feels like part of you. Many come from our experiences, where we created beliefs, and then respond to similar situations in the same way, out of fear, danger or a need for protection.

Do any of those descriptions feel open or expansive to you? There can be no 'danger' if we've learned strategies to use time and time again for every situation. Our role is to use EAM to release those patterns and see them for what they are – forms of protection.

Self-sabotage

The biggest pattern we see in personal development is self-sabotage. We see it all the time (and spent many years doing it ourselves!). Again, self-sabotage is a pattern of coping. It's a way of unconsciously destroying something that could be so promising, to allow everything in our life to remain predictable, within the status quo! The unconscious need to be in control creates a sense of safety even if what you aim to maintain is damaging to you. It's a sure-fire way to keep manifesting exactly the same thing.

How many times have you heard someone say, '*I haven't had time for that, I've been too busy.*' Then you find them on the sofa watching TV. The issue here is twofold: (a) they say those words, which means the Law of Attraction will keep on bringing it to them, and (b) they're spending most of their time feeling overwhelmed and therefore unable to take action on everything they have to get done. So, they waste time watching TV. This creates a pattern and eventually a self-fulfilling prophecy, which will continue until they do something to step outside of it. Have you ever found yourself in something like this? In your case, this means it's time to EAM.

Element 2 Exercise – Letting Go of Self-sabotage Patterns

We could create an endless list of self-sabotage patterns. Let's start with some of the most common ones that stand in our way. In Step 1, ask the sway out loud which of these statements are true for you. For example, '*Do I have a pattern of sabotaging myself?*' If you sway 'yes' on any, work through the Five Steps. Here are a few to get you started. Feel free to add your own, or work on anything you know gets in your way.

DO I HAVE A PATTERN OF …	SUGGESTED STEP 5 STATEMENT (I AM ready to allow …)
Sabotaging myself?	myself to stay aligned to the path that I AM on and embrace whatever the universe delivers to me. I AM my own best friend and always make decisions for my highest good …
Never starting on important things I want to do?	myself to easily get everything done, in the right way, at the right time. I get all my important tasks done first and enjoy them all …
Feeling overwhelmed or confused?	myself to have clarity and calmness, to get everything done easily and receive inspired ideas …
Looking at outside situations instead of within?	feel empowered, knowing everything outside is a reflection of within …
Preventing good things coming into my life?	and accept good things to come into my life, through every conversation, opportunity and doorway …
Allowing other people to treat me badly?	only the right people into my life. I AM worthy and I AM my number one priority …
Comparing myself to others?	and accept that I AM worthwhile, deserving and creating a life I love for me …
Focusing on lack?	myself to embrace and understand my life is abundant in all areas and I AM grateful for everything I've received …
Having to do everything perfectly?	that I can make mistakes, knowing that I've learned from the experience …
Procrastination?	myself to be motivated and focused on what's right for me ….

Element 3 –
Transform Your Emotions and Vibration

We're still working into your aura as we move from the mental to the emotional layer. Here we investigate how your emotions impact your everyday life. We'll refer to the emotional scale (see p. 97), and let go of addictive or negative emotional patterns that form habitual ways of feeling. Again, this is a glimpse of what's possible as you can also use EAM to work on emotional entanglements with others, emotional abuse, overwhelm, stress, anxiety, depression, building confidence and self-esteem. Together, we'll raise your emotional set point, creating high-vibe emotions so you're more consistently in a positive place.

We used to believe that emotions were an outcome of our thinking. Many of us were brought up to ignore emotions and only trust our logical thinking mind. By now, you know your emotions are powerful, and that they're something *you can* control. It's a wonderful mix of energetic, physiological and psychological influences, from our heart and brain. By learning how to consistently raise your emotional set point, you'll begin to see your life change and expand for the better.

Emotional health is how you feel day-to-day. We want to get you reconnected to your body and your emotions as they're one of the key ways we experience life. Everything we do is because we want to feel good or at least better than we do right now. We'd never consciously do anything to ourselves that makes us feel worse. Yet, you can see how we're unconsciously doing this all the time, simply through a lack of knowledge.

It's our job to choose to feel good in every moment, no matter what's happening outside. We're meant to feel good! Remember everything in the universe is designed to grow, expand and be in alignment. How amazing will it be to feel like that every day? In EAM, we call that alignment.

Emotional health means more self-esteem, confidence and sense of worth. You no longer react with knee-jerk responses, anxiety or panic to the events that occur in your life. Instead, you're an emotionally safe person to be around – you're calming and patient because you feel secure with your own emotions and can express yourself in healthy, assertive ways.

Understanding Our Confusing Emotions

Emotions can be confusing. From our time in the womb and as young children we learn through our senses, using touch and sound, feeling emotions and the energy around us to 'read' other people. This is called emotional intelligence, meaning we're able to solve emotion-related problems, and it develops way before verbal communication. We rely on other people to keep us safe, so we need to be able to read and understand their cues. We trust these methods of communication because they're unmistakable.

Imagine we had an emotion like love demonstrated by our parents through stress, anger or irritability. How confusing for a small child to have someone saying, 'I love you' through gritted teeth. Their inner senses would be telling them one thing while simultaneously listening to someone they trust. In this situation, we're always taught to defer to the judgement of parents. Kids think their inner feelings are wrong because mum or whoever says that it's something else. For this reason, we can also become confused about our real emotions and feel unable to trust ourselves as we grow older.

It's through a lifetime of these experiences, that we disconnect from our own guidance (positive and negative) and let other people explain our feelings! For example, if you were jumping around and having fun in the kitchen and someone shouted at you to stop because you were playing near a hot oven, in that moment you perceive it's wrong to be playing and feeling excited. Meanwhile, they just wanted to keep you safe.

Sometimes people find it hard to engage or connect to any emotions at all. If you experience numbness instead of emotions, there's nothing wrong with you; it could mean you spent long periods of time suppressing your emotions; an energy reversal was created when you expressed emotion and had it shut down; a situation caused you to disconnect from your body; or medication, or other energy toxins. But it's all just energy, which means it can be changed. During this element, drink plenty of water, get lots of sleep and rest. Remember that everything we unleash and transform has the equal and opposite amount of energy at the other end of the scale. As you release this numbness, you're in for one hell of a ride into love and joy.

In general, we are rarely raised to be joyful and happy or to do what we feel is right. We're constrained by so many rules and other people's ideas of what we 'should' and 'shouldn't' conform to, when there's really only one universal rule: to always do what makes us happy or experience love! Imagine what the world will be like when we all live that way. The irony is, we need positive emotions to create the life we want, so choose to feel better.

As you feel more positive, you'll naturally attract more positive things to you. If you catch yourself saying, '*I just need to do … before I can be happy … or fall in love …*' then you have some EAM to do, as that JUST is a resistance. Everything is always about how you feel first, in order for it to come. With EAM, our intention is to change our internal energetic, mental and emotional set points so that the messages being sent around the body and out in our energy are something we'd choose.

Transform Your Emotions and Your Reality

To change our reality, we have to practise feeling good. This can feel hard if you're still in the old paradigm way of thinking, observing what's happening now instead of consciously creating with your energy. If you continue to talk, think or take actions based on what's happening now, you'll only get more of the same.

If you feel resistance about something you perceive, you're unable to change what you see while you feel that way. Your work is to note what you feel or think and begin to transform your life. To create change we have to accept that it's down to us to change how we feel. Emotions are energy – they can transform in an instant. As you use EAM on this you're rewiring your energy, too. So, you're transforming your own perceptions of reality in an instant, as well.

Element 3 Exercise – Rise Up the Emotional Scale

Pay attention to your emotions, what you're feeling. Are you finding yourself stuck in a habitual way of feeling that no longer serves you? Are you seeking experiences that validate your current emotions and feed more of them? As a powerful clearing exercise, you can use the emotional scale from page 97. In Step 1, ask your sway how many of each of these emotions you're carrying using the numbers method. You can then work to transform them all at once so they're no longer in your aura. You can also check in with this exercise as a daily routine.

Align to more of the positive emotions above the neutral line. Really *feel* what they're like in your body. What size, shape and colour are they? Allow them to expand and fill your energy. Connect back to them often.

Element 4 –
Transform Your Physical Health

We're ready to start changing our physical health, working our way into the layers of your aura related to the physical and etheric. Changing our physical health with EAM is so much easier now we've reduced the spiritual, mental and emotional imprints held in the energy field, which have been impacting it.

Traditionally in the West, we've been brought up to believe that our physical body is mechanical. It's a machine that operates different systems functionally independent of one another, and you can affect one area of our physiology, or cut something out, without it affecting something elsewhere in the body. Now, however, modern medicine is starting to recognize the mind–body connection. While they're yet to be as open to the Eastern medicinal practices, our intention is that one day EAM and other energy tools will be the norm.

We have the power to shape and change our physical health, and by working with the energy first we can prevent many physical health conditions from even arising! That is our biggest wish: to empower each and every one of us to take care of our health on every level.

Your physical body is the beautiful vessel that you use to define who you are. It's the most manifested form of our aura. Your physical body reflects your thoughts, feelings and emotions. The size, shape, skin tone, colour of your tongue, the thin bits, fat bits, the toned bits and wobbly bits are *all* a manifestation of your energy. Our physical health is created by the practiced thoughts and feelings we have. Our physical body reflects our alignment. The ill health and disease we experience is a reflection of our misalignment. This can be a difficult thing to hear for some, and people often ask: *'What about those who are born with a hereditary condition, or that young child who developed an illness?'*

We are not pointing the finger, blaming or judging anyone. It's one of those moments to step into the new paradigm. When we recognize that everything is energy, including illnesses that we call inherited, it means we have the power to change them. If we simply accept the idea it's inherited, we give up as if there's nothing we can do. We once again lose our power. When we are actually all powerful. We wish we had space to share all the stories of physical health conditions, symptoms and mystifying recoveries seen when people have used EAM. Are we promising miraculous healing when doing energy work? Of course not. Are we saying people may find relief, transformation, healing, understanding, release of guilt, blame, shame, anger, frustration and feeling of powerlessness around it? Yes. Will that allow the body to get into a healing space? Yes. Who knows what changes may occur in the physical symptoms of their illness, their mental or emotional condition or how they live their life? Surely any relief on any level is better than none. It's a far more powerful way to approach it, don't you agree?

The development of our physical body began at conception and throughout our time in the womb. Many of our energetic patterns and potential are set in place from our parents. The blueprint of our physical body is created at conception, however we can still influence it. What an extraordinary journey our energy and physical bodies go on before we take our first breath. Much of our lives are shaped by the thoughts, feelings and emotions of our parents during conception and pregnancy.

Disease (DIS-EASE) in the body is simply an energetic manifestation of some area of our lives that is out of alignment. If you've manifested a disease, it means there'll be a corresponding resistant vibration of energy. Our physical bodies are the most manifested form of our energy, it's our role to take care of this 'container'.

If you feel sick, tired, exhausted, eat too much sugar or fat, or are dehydrated, suffer from a lack of sleep, forget to exercise or find time to relax, you'll feel more out of sync. This means you'll also be keeping what you want to manifest away from you. In addition to all of the elements already explored, we're also affected by diet, wifi, chemicals, our physical environment, diseases and our genetics. All of these are just different types of energy. So, if everything is energy, we have the power to influence it with EAM, even if they're 'manifested' illnesses or conditions!

To change situations physically, we need to maintain a habit of positive vibration on a physical level. If we're feeling tired, have headaches, body pain or any uncomfortable physical sensation, it's an indication that we're out of alignment in some area of our life.

Our energy system has been subtly communicating to us for a while. The reason that chronic or acute physical health conditions are expressed is that we ignored the energetic messages when they were on the mental, emotional or etheric level of our aura. It can also be that we've had an energetic shock significant enough to create changes in our energy and on a physical level.

When we understand the metaphysical meanings of pain or illness in the body, you can see the connection between your consciousness and your physical body. It's a map of your energy, thoughts, beliefs and emotions. The tissues and organs in our body are little energetic storage places for emotions and memories. A book we highly recommend is *Metaphysical Anatomy* by Evette Rose (CreateSpace, 2013), which will give you clues as to the messages from your body, which you can then use EAM to work through.

Our physical bodies can be changed by emotions we experience. They store and have memories at a molecular level. So, neither mind nor body can be treated without the other being affected. This is exactly what we're doing with EAM. We're releasing the energy, emotions, memories and thoughts from our aura and physical body. They're all connected anyway! By releasing this resistance, we're allowing our bodies to heal on a physical level. In turn, this transforms our ability to manifest on a physical level.

Remember how the aura and chakras are communicating with the body through the autonomic nervous systems. Our nervous system is always reading what's happening in our aura, and if an energy imprint, thought, belief or emotion has continued for long enough, it will create a physiological health response. Like the last snowflake falling on a thick layer of snow, it's the build-up that came before which causes the cascade. In the same way that it can take time for multiple imprints to develop into a health condition, it will also take a multi-angle approach when working on it with EAM. While it's easy to get the body into a healing state, healing physically requires changes on all levels, including the environment, thoughts, beliefs, emotions, food, sleep, people, space to create more flow – clearing these all aids in a faster healing.

Numbing Out

We explored earlier in the book the impact of stress on physical health; it's the precursor to almost every condition. Of course, we know stress is resistance, and is the physiological impact of what's happening within our biofield. One of the most common ways that we now deal with stress in our modern world is to turn to external substances such as alcohol, tobacco or drugs to relieve it. We numb ourselves in so many ways to prevent us from *really* connecting with ourselves – it may be food, drink, drugs or prescription medication, TV, social media or shopping. These all create a disconnect in our lives. They create additional resistance in our physical bodies and, in some cases, reversals in our energy. So, we can be in a constant reversed energy state because of the substances we put into our body.

What foods do you notice you're addicted to? What substances could you choose to eliminate from your diet in order to improve your energy flow? Use the sway to help you find them, and then release the powerful emotions, patterns or addictions connected to them with the Five Steps of EAM. By doing this, you'll allow your body to be more energized, feel aligned and vibrate at a higher frequency.

Physical Exercise

Although we all know we're 'meant' to exercise, sometimes we feel pretty uninspired to do so. There are lots of ways we can get some regular exercise that can be fun instead of

regimented, and there are many reasons to exe
from an energy standpoint, it increases the mov
through the body. It helps us to sleep, improves our ...
metabolism, digestion, controls weight, reduces the risk of
diseases and can lower blood pressure.

There are different types of exercise that may support you.
Aerobic exercise helps the heart, strength training helps the
muscles, and flexibility training helps joints remain bendy!
Since you want to reduce any resistance, you may have to
begin exercising and also find the right exercises that your
body wants you to do, and that you'll enjoy doing. You can
use the Five Steps to release resistance to doing the exercises.
Start by using Step 1 to ask your sway which type of exercise
it really wants or needs.

Transforming Ill Health

With EAM, you can change your health before you've
manifested a physical condition by honouring and nurturing
your physical body. Having spent many years working in
complementary health, we can only share what we know has
worked for us and our clients. Please seek your own advice
when making changes to your physical body; the information
given here will never replace a medical expert, your doctor,
consultant or mental health professional. You know your body
best, so please seek your own advice and make the best, most
informed choice for you.

However, within EAM we do have a step-by-step approach
to begin dealing with your physical health conditions. You
already have much of it here to assist you. One way to begin is
to use the bubble method we shared in Chapter 6 (see p. 164),
to systematically work through any health condition, even
simply releasing the pain, aches and symptoms in your body.

The more you do, the more coherent state you create, and the quicker the body can heal. There are many ways to use EAM for your physical health, and this is a great start.

Your Health Story

We all have a story about every aspect of our life. Do you have a health story, a 'reason' why you're unable to move forward in life? Why you may be a different weight to what you want? Why you have trouble sleeping, exercising, _____ (you fill in the blank)? In its simplest terms, it's the reason (excuse) you use for maintaining incongruent energy around your health and wellbeing. While you hold that story it will continue to be true for you, so let's lose the story and create something new. Let's explore this with EAM in the following exercise.

Element 4 Exercise – Transform Your Physical Health

It takes more than one imprint to manifest a physical condition, so there'll be more than one area of resistance that has contributed to it. These questions are a starting point. We suggest getting a big sheet of paper, using the bubble method (see p. 164) and mind-mapping the answers. Use your sway to answer these questions, as you're likely to get a different answer to what you believe consciously.

- Look at when it began. What was happening? Who was there? How old were you?

- Look at the emotions you experienced back then. How did you feel about it then and now?
- Who, if anyone, do you blame for your current health condition, and why?
- Look at your thoughts about your health condition. Do you believe it will heal? Do you believe it was inherited? Do you believe there is nothing that can be done?
- What are your regular symptoms of this condition? Describe how they feel in your energy field. List them all, even if you only feel them sometimes.
- What does this prevent you from doing?
- What does it allow you to do, get or receive?

Using EAM, work on each of the answers you find to the questions.

You can use this process to work on different conditions; work on each separately. Even the most serious conditions can be helped with EAM.

If working with other health professionals while using EAM, you can to let them know what you're doing to support yourself alongside your medical care.

This process may take a while, but it's so worth it to allow your body to heal. The big secret is to rest after you do this work, too!

Once you have done this we invite you to write your new story.

What DO you want your health to be like? Write it in the present tense. Write, picture, imagine and align to your new positive healthy state.

Element 5 –
Creating the Right Physical Environment

We've explored our inner world by looking at the soul, so now let's take a look at your life as we consider our influence in the life outside of us – in our environment, relationships and creating our dream lifestyle. It's much simpler than you think. We promise.

Creating the right physical environment is about working with the space around you. Energetically, we're still looking at the physical and etheric levels of your auric field as you start to expand your light into the world. Is your physical space supporting or depleting you energetically? Your vibration is massively influenced by the space you're in (and the other people in it). If your space is unsupportive, it impacts your frequency more than you know.

Your LIFE is your world around you.

Other than working on our physical bodies, this is the first time we've worked with real manifested stuff – solid objects! But this is more than manifesting new things. It's about alignment with our physical environment, spending time in a space we adore because it raises our vibration. As human beings, we're designed to observe what's in front of us. It's so easy to see what's around us and judge it – if we're spending our time somewhere we'd rather not be, we're putting out resistant energy. If you live in a home that makes you feel ashamed, with tatty walls or décor that makes you cringe, then you're taken out of alignment. You need to clear up your vibration and the energy in the space you have using EAM, then take some practical action to change it, love it and make sure it's supporting you. This also creates the right vibration to manifest the new space you truly want.

Why Change Our Physical Space?

Our physical bodies are the most manifested form of our energy; everything that comes into our physical space is impacting us through our aura. Depending on our vibrational frequency, mood and receptive state, our aura can expand between 2 and 20 metres away. Therefore, what and who you spend time with impacts your vibration. In the same way we're clearing our aura to allow more 'good' to flow in, we have to do the same within our workplace and home. If we want to start manifesting into our physical life, the physical space has to be a vibrational match to it.

If you live in a shoebox full of clutter with no space around you, there's no space to grow and expand; you're literally restricted by the space and what's influencing your vibration. Consider the type of newspapers, magazines and books you read. Do they inspire you or bring you down? Do you listen to the news on the TV or radio? Do you need it? Are you in environments that support you? Do you have enough daylight? Fresh air?

We begin, of course, with aligning ourselves to what we have right now – by transforming any resistance to what lies around us. This doesn't mean settling – it *does* mean getting your vibration in a good place (or more) about what you have, especially if you know you often gripe about your current home.

In order to create, we have to love what we have. While you may be waiting for your dream home to arrive, it's important to feel great about where you live. Go around your house and stand in each room; notice if you feel a change in your vibration, notice the thoughts and emotions that come up for you. Use the Five Steps of EAM to release any resistance you feel. By doing this, you'll allow yourself to be in a more high-frequency state when in that space, which will raise your alignment level.

Your Dream Home

It's time to get creative. If you've done the visualization meditation (see p. 143), perhaps you've 'seen' your dream home. Or get yourself into that state with Step 5 and ask your sway some questions about it. What does it look like? What does each room look like? What colours are on the walls? Is it an old home or a new build? What's outside or near to your home? Do you want to be in the countryside or live in the city? Maybe you live in your perfect house already and you know it needs a revamp! Start planning the changes to your space. Make an EAM vision board for the type of house you want to create.

A Note About Feng Shui

Feng Shui is the Chinese practice of harmonizing ourselves with the surrounding environment, by creating energy flow in the physical space to influence the flow of Qi in different areas of our lives. Classical Feng Shui is the world's oldest and most comprehensive 'environmental design' method and is increasingly crucial in our modern world as it enables us to create homes that support our wellness instead of draining environments. Our good friend Sarah McAllister, founder of the Feng Shui Agency in London, explains, 'When aligning with our highest aspirations, passions and desires, what many of us never consider is that we're already being profoundly influenced, and in some cases sabotaged *by, the design of our homes and buildings. Each home and building has a unique energy imprint which is caused by many factors: the type of land and environment the building sits on, orientation of the building, placement of doors and windows, garden design, colours used internally and layout of furniture and symbolic artwork.'*

Feng Shui is all about organizing your space for optimum flow, and you can do much of this yourself by using the Five Steps of EAM, with additional assistance from a Feng Shui expert like Sarah, if you so wish.

The Energy in Your Home

Just like everything else in life, any physical space holds its own Qi too. There can be parts of your home that are in flow, some in resistance, and some in reversal. Imagine someone has had a big argument or some drama has happened in a particular room in the past. It leaves an energy imprint there. Have you ever walked into a house where someone lived alone for many years, or a room where a fight had broken out? The energy of the room still remains. Walk around your home and simply ask your sway if there's any resistance to clear in each room. If 'yes', follow the Five Steps to release and align to a better flow of Qi.

It's also important to know that our environment is a representation of what's happening in our own Qi, so if you're living in a house of mess and chaos, your energy field will be the same. Likewise, when your space is clean, clear, tidy and free-flowing, your energy field will be, too. So clear up the clutter, remove unwanted items and zen your space ASAP.

If you have clutter in rooms in your house or where you sleep, you'll have a cluttered mind that prevents inspired thoughts and ideas to be given to you. If it's in your bedroom, it will also affect your sleep and your ability to heal. If you've no space in your home because it's full of old stuff you have hanging around (from your past) then you literally and metaphorically have no space to allow the new in.

Think about an object that you 'keep' because it holds memories or energy for you. Is it a memory of love or does it take you out of alignment every time you look at it? Are you holding onto it for fear of loss, or holding onto the past? Who does it serve by hanging on to it? Who else would benefit from it? How can you transform your clutter into money? Sway on the objects you need to let go. You can sell unwanted or unneeded items and will be amazed at how much spare 'cash' is sitting around you.

Other powerful principles to explore further in the Energy Evolution are simple Feng Shui concepts, clearing the energy vortexes and lines through our home, sound cleansing and protecting against EMFs, wifi, cleaning products and other materials that affect our vibrational frequency.

Element 5 Exercise – Is Everything Supporting You?

Part of your job in creating the right physical environment for you is to clear some space and make sure that everything that's left is supporting your energy. We want to ensure that you can at least enjoy the space you have, because that is the best way to manifest something new or make meaningful changes to your home anyway.

Your Computer, Phone or Tablet

Technology is a huge energetic distraction, so this is a great place to start. It's essential to carry out regular housekeeping on your technology and here are some suggestions:

- Check your computer is working properly. Does it load when you open it and connect well to the internet?
- Are all your computer files in order so that you can find everything easily? Organize them thoroughly and delete those no longer needed.
- Go through your inbox, and delete old emails and unsubscribe from lists you no longer want to receive (you can also sway on which to unsubscribe from).
- Social media contacts: delete people you no longer wish to connect with and connect to those you do.

Clear the Clutter

Many of us have accumulated too much stuff over the years and it can feel overwhelming to address. We suggest you diary some time each week to tackle one element of your clutter and you'll soon gain momentum, see a difference in your surroundings and feel it in your vibrational energy.

- Do you need to empty drawers, cupboards or wardrobes?
- Get rid of old paperwork that is no longer needed.
- Let go of memorabilia that brings up resistant emotions.
- Does your space feel welcoming or overcrowded?
- Does furniture need to move or go?

Use the sway to enable you to decide what to let go and what to keep. Release any resistance using the Five Steps of EAM and align to living in a harmonious space.

Element 6 –
Revolutionizing Your Relationships

In this element, we're still working on your life, taking another expansive step out to the emotional level of your aura. This enables you to connect to a place of love in all of your key relationships with yourself and others.

Relationships are one of the most powerful pulls on our emotions. From a young age, we use relationships to establish meaning in our lives. We learn everything about relationships from parents or caregivers because they're all we know, and we're dependent on them to literally keep us alive. Depending on who they are and how they behaved, a lot of this will have shaped how you are as an adult.

Many families are unconscious of their behaviours, verbal and non-verbal communication, or the impact of their actions. This means they are unconsciously operating patterns learned and observed in their childhood, which influence how they live, connect and interact. People behave as if they're powerless – they point the finger, place blame, and believe everything outside of them has made their life this way. They're yet to understand that they create their reality and it can change by transforming their thoughts, emotions and actions.

This way of forming relationships is the old paradigm way of thinking. What we want to do here is stop perpetuating that story and let go of beliefs, thoughts, emotions and patterns that are disempowering us. This way we become responsible for our own lives and what's happening to us, and also take responsibility for changing it.

Why Relationships Play With Our Energy

We learn how to behave in relationships before the age of three. If we witnessed negative dynamics, we'll have internalized thoughts, words, feelings, actions and behaviours at an unconscious level, because we absorbed and soaked up the environment like sponges in our early years.

As we get older, the relationships we developed from watching our parents or caregivers extends to siblings, friends and family, teachers, colleagues, boyfriends, girlfriends, husbands and wives; until we repeat the cycle again perhaps with our own children. These important and powerful relationships have great significance in our lives. They're often a drive behind what we do, which means any unhealthy interactions impact our lives and theirs on a daily basis.

Many of the 'issues' we have in relationships come from a feeling of lack; we think that we're short or scarce of something – that somehow, we're not enough, or someone isn't doing, being or having enough! We unconsciously look for others to fill the gaps we feel are missing in us. With EAM, we talk about abundant thinking, and this is more than just money in the bank. We mean time, money, food, love, kindness, freedom, support, attention and connection. Imagine being able to let the other people in your life off the hook, as you become your own source of everything because it's all just energy. When you know that this is true about everything in life, you no longer want or need to rely on others to be that source of anything for you, because you trust the infinite abundance of all of them coming from the universe!

Look at the important relationships in your life. Where are you expecting others to meet your needs, fill your gaps or give something to you to make you feel happy? Use the Five ps of EAM to sway on what you have, who with and how you may be draining your relationship. By aligning yourself to being able to receive these abundant resources with Step 5, you can free yourself and others.

Be Free of the Energy Drama

Many relationships operate within an unconscious dynamic known as the Karpman drama triangle. It explains the interactions where no one is at fault, everyone else is to blame, and no one is accepting responsibility for their words, thoughts or actions (and, we'd add, their alignment!). We've all fallen into this at some point and might default back to it when under stress. We're often completely unconscious that it's even going on. You'll find that most people believe that life happens to them; if something good happens they believe it's luck. If something bad happens, it's someone else's fault!

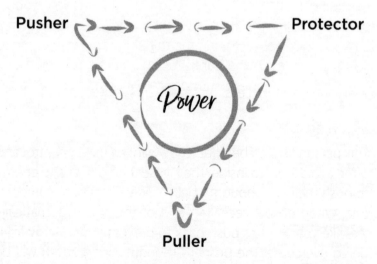

The EAM Energy Drama

Within EAM we call this the Energy Drama because it's about the push, pull and protector movements of energy, which keeps this drama cycling. The communication always looks 'honest', yet there's often a hidden and unconscious motive to it, so the interactions are energetically communicating the hidden meaning. The drama unfolds as people miscommunicate verbally and energetically with pushing energy, drawing from others and placing blame. This is all coming from a place of lack, a belief that to win someone else has to lose.

This drama triangle is one that we play out unconsciously. We often have a default position as **puller**, **pusher** or **protector**, and we can flit between them depending who we're talking to. We believe this is normal, as most relationships work in this way, reinforced by soap operas/films/books/newspaper stories. The old paradigm, based on control and taking away other peoples' power, takes us out of alignment. With EAM, you need to be conscious, be fully responsible for your life and be in alignment. We call this your place of power.

These interactions are always a two-way thing. Remember two energies moving in opposite directions create tension and resistance. It's a constant push–pull power play where everyone gets lost. Let's look at the three roles.

The Pusher
This person likes to be right. They want to feel in control and often avoid looking inside. They'll use their power and energy to push their will, thoughts, beliefs or feelings onto someone else. When on the receiving end of this, you automatically feel like you want to push back to prevent your energy from being overcome. The pusher's thoughts and pattern will be to blame and to provoke conflict, always believing they're justified. They like to be in authority.

The Puller

A puller is the one who has been attacked by the pusher. When you meet a veteran puller, you'll feel them pulling you in like you're circling down a plughole. These people want their own way and will glean support from others without directly asking. The puller draws energy from a protector (and everyone else around them too); they're often giving their power away by blaming everyone else for their situation. The puller wants to be seen as innocent and helpless. Secretly, everyone wants to be in the position of the puller, because they're free of responsibility and looked after, and everyone else takes the blame.

The Protector

The protector is the one who gets to be a hero. You'll find them riding in to save the day for a puller. This is the soul aim of the protector. They get their high by being the saviour and being relied upon by the puller for emotional support. They'll often intervene with the pusher to protect the puller, and feel obligated to do this even if they loathe doing it. They want to help and they feel guilty if they don't. Most of their support is given begrudgingly with an underlying expectation that at some point in the future the puller owes them. This is often a co-dependent energy dynamic where neither person is happy. Their energy demands credit for the support that they give.

Can you see how all of these are disempowering? All of these push and pull us from one frequency state to another. All the time, our energy, attention and focus is taken away from the important topic of changing our life.

So, how do you step into your power? Remember that you have a choice. By using EAM, you can work your way through all of these interactions by recognizing that any energy, thoughts, beliefs or emotions that come up are *about you*. When you can own that and commit to doing the work on yourself first, you can step into your power. This is about coming from the new paradigm and recognizing your energy state before you communicate.

Finding New Love

If you're on the search for a new relationship, whether that be a friend or partner, you need to transform any resistant thoughts, beliefs and emotions you've held about your relationships from the past. If you hold a belief that all men are assholes or that all women are after your money, what do you think you'll attract into the next relationship? To change what you attract in your relationships, first change yourself. By changing your energy and past stories you allow in the possibility for what you want.

Get clear with yourself what beliefs, patterns or emotions you hold. Align yourself to allowing in only the best possible experiences for yourself in a new relationship. Follow the Five Steps of EAM and use the sway to define the important traits you want to attract.

Unconditional Love

As you can see, our relationships are often pretty complicated with so many well-meaning intentions, emotions and unrealistic expectations on how other people 'should' behave.

So many relationships are built on *conditional* love, meaning 'if you behave a certain way, I will love you! If you don't, then I won't!' Although we never say that out loud, we certainly act that way! For many, this is how we were raised to behave by our parents. Conditional love teaches us many lessons from a young age, which create many of the patterns and resistances we experience as adults.

Look at the way you connect and communicate with others. Where are you being conditional with your love? Where are you closing yourself off from love and flow? Use the Five Steps of EAM to work on any resistance you feel about them. By aligning yourself to more unconditional love, you'll receive more of it from life and those people around you.

Real Self-love

Finally, we need to create an amazing relationship with ourselves first and foremost, by taking responsibility for ourselves. By that, we mean being in alignment, loving ourselves. Why live a life that is dependent on someone else being in a good mood and loving you in order to feel good? We want to be able to feel love in any and all circumstances because without that we've nothing to give or share with anyone else anyway!

There is so much more within the Energy Evolution to explore with relationships, such as issues around sex, intimacy, hidden roles of the masculine and feminine, working with parenting, family constellations, healing old family trauma, dealing with co-dependency and narcissism. You can also look at learning to communicate with love, truth and transparency, working with your inner child, loving yourself and finding your true love relationship.

For us, learning to love yourself is what EAM is all about. Whether you call it flow, love or alignment, it's all one and the same thing. Our connection to love is being in alignment; when we have our own connection to our source, we're connected to the infinite, abundant source of love. Why wait to receive it from people or other outside forces? We have it within us, always!

Element 6 Exercise –
Time to Release the Drama

Using the sway, explore which of the three energy archetypes you are most likely to be. Ask,

- Am I a **pusher**?
- Am I a **puller**?
- Am I a **protector**?

Although it's common to be all three, you'll have a tendency to be one of them more than the others. You can also ask the sway which one of these you are in relation to key people in your life, and use the Five Steps of EAM to release this archetypal role you play so you can align to being in your power.

Pay attention to your interactions with others. Learn to recognize when you're slipping into these energy dynamics, and use EAM to release habits and behaviours so you can change the dynamic of your relationships and reclaim your power.

Element 7 – Living Your Dream Lifestyle

This is the last part of re-finding your life. We're at the mental level of our aura, and it's time to expand our knowledge, skills and expertise. It's about enriching ourselves and our life experience with things we previously only dreamt of.

Life is meant to be fun, yet enjoyment often gets put to the bottom of the list. When was the last time you truly let your hair down and had some fun? When was the last time you played bat and ball or rolled down a hill like a small child? This element is about that childlike nature. Life is about more than work, being a parent or partner – life is about how you're spending your time. Are you enjoying what you do?

From an energetic perspective, what we experience as fun is actually the feeling of alignment or being in flow. When we're rolling down that hill, we're truly connected to our inner selves, and enjoying that moment in time without resistance. That is what the feeling of alignment is.

Fun and recreation are an essential part of human life. Anything can be fun because it's all about our vibration. All too often, the childlike nature has been drummed out of us. We've also curbed it by our own perceptions. Maybe your parents yelled at you to stop doing something – *'Don't climb on the sofa!'* What this created was a sense of doubt. You disconnected and stopped allowing yourself to have fun and be spontaneous.

If you have children, please pay attention to the times that you find yourself saying, 'No', or 'Stop!' Ask yourself if you really need them to stop. Could you let your 'adult' go in and join them instead? Allow them to experience that sense of joy, excitement, spontaneity and fun in their connection to life. Help them to stay children and create happier memories.

Take a look at the silent beliefs that pop up whenever you're about to have fun. What are the voices you hear? What do they say? What did you hear growing up? Follow the Five Steps of EAM to work through them, align to having fun, playing, laughter and feeling excited.

Your Ideal Lifestyle

This part of the journey is also about enjoying the lifestyle you want. We know life means more than materialistic elements, yet there's no shame in enjoying the good stuff either. If you were allowing yourself to live the life of your dreams right now, what would you be doing with your time today? Would you be on holiday? At the spa? It can be so tempting to hold off starting to live the life you want because of practicalities, or by thinking about your current life. The whole idea with manifesting is to align your thoughts, words, beliefs, behaviours and actions. All of this is essential *before* it will begin to manifest.

Our ideal lifestyle probably has us resting a little bit more than we do right now. As much as we talk about taking action, there's also magic in the relaxation, in sitting still and doing nothing. We're conditioned to think that the only way to create is to 'do'. The truth is, the benefits of laughter, enjoying yourself and getting in the flow of being in the moment far outweigh action taking. However, you need to flow between the two, to take time to relax and at other times to take action.

Have you ever noticed that when you go on holiday miracles seem to happen? As you relax, you stop putting out any contradictory energy. You no longer create new thoughts or feelings, or move the goalposts. When you take time out to relax – physically and energetically – the universe can find you and deliver what you've been asking for. Fun, laughter and relaxation expand your energy, open you to receive, and make you more attractive.

Your Creative Energy

You are an expanding being and developing your knowledge is another way you continue to grow. When did you last embark on learning something totally new for you? The process of learning and education engages our left brain – the sensible, practical, logical part. We need it to be on top form, as much as we need to engage our right (creative) brain.

To keep expanding, we need to challenge ourselves: to learn and acquire new skills that stretch us.

Creativity, art or crafts puts you in the space of being in your right brain, which naturally connects to a higher source. Allow yourself the time and space to be in flow. Finding a way to switch off your normal mental activity and be in that open, creative space allows the inspired thoughts and ideas to drop in.

The state of creative energy is a powerful place. This is where we access the potential energy we use to manifest. The more you connect to your creativity, the more quickly things will manifest for you. Creativity is more than painting or knitting; it can also be your work. How can you, or do you, use your creative energy in your everyday life? It's more about the energy of what you're doing than the task itself. This is about you being in that new flow, that new source of creativity, the new manifestation.

Element 7 Exercise – Do Something for You

Use the Five Steps of EAM to release the resistance to doing the activities that are part of your dream life. Pick three things you'd love to do but that you always say you're too busy for. Pay attention to all the energy, thoughts, beliefs, patterns and emotions that surface when you think about what stands in your way. Use the bubble method to work through it all and align to allow the vibration of them into your life. Then go out and take action. Book them in. Tell the universe you're serious about changing your life. Then watch the magic unfold.

Element 8 – Expanding Your Money, Wealth and Abundance

This is where we begin to create the real magic. The key elements of our soul and our life are in alignment. Now it's time for us to explore and expand our newly aligned selves into our expression of work in the world. That means finding a way to be in alignment with the money and wealth you receive so that you can use it to make a meaningful impact. We'll define your passion and purpose, enabling you to get clarity on how you can make an impact.

> *Your WORK is your interaction with the wider world.*

It's time to connect to the abundance of wealth. Now we're working in the outer levels of our energy bodies; we've connected to the sources of wealth inside, so now we can tap into those around us. Money is like everything else – it's just energy. Usually, by now, the 'need' we previously had for money has disappeared. You've already done most of the work to shift your money story. You see that money is never about the money; it's about what you think the money will bring you.

The meaning of money and abundant resources is ingrained in us from birth. We're brought up in an old paradigm system that believes that money = power. We inherently believe that it's the source of our power. We also believe that wealthy people have more time and therefore scarcity of time signifies a lack of abundance and vice versa. We believe that more money = more time = more freedom. We see happy, smiling pictures of wealthy people having free time with friends. So, we connect money to friends, fun and happiness. With all of these important and implicit meanings connected to money, no wonder it means so much.

In the new paradigm, you know these are all limitless resources. They're all sources of energy, freely available that you can tap into. No one owns them.

We've also been taught happiness is dependent on having money. It's true that having money does make life feel easier. However, if you ask anyone what they want money for, whether it's a car, house, holiday or to pay the bills, when you ask, 'and *why* do you want the _____?' it usually is the same answer. What they actually want is the *feeling* they believe their desire will bring them – freedom, peace of mind, love, happiness. Here's the universal joke, you can have those without needing the money first, by being in alignment. To get the money, you have to feel those emotions first anyway. So it's a win–win.

For many people, the issue around money is that they have a tidal wave of energy flowing in the opposite direction when it comes to abundance. This is because we have so many conflicting beliefs, thoughts, feelings, patterns and emotions around this issue. These are often created at a young age and through significant events in our lives. Very often money has caused conflict in relationships. We learned patterns in our families about what we think we can or can't create.

Think about the energy of money in general. Are people in alignment when handling it, talking about it or spending it? The vibration of money for many is low frequency. Money is an energy that wants to be free-flowing. Imagine for a moment that money is a child; would you speak to a child in the way you do about money? Imagine all the pressure being put on money to perform. What a weight it has to carry. What if you could become a money-cleaner, changing the frequency of money into and out of your bank, purse or wallet? As you free up the energy of money, more money will flow to you.

Abundance is a mindset, which means money and wealth is also a mindset. Like all manifesting, it takes some gathering of momentum by giving our focused energy, thoughts, feelings and actions to see it manifest in our reality.

As you know, before you can manifest money, you have to think and feel abundantly, habitually as a way of life. One or two days of thinking abundantly will not make you a millionaire!

We have a secret to tell you: we are born to be abundant! It's a way of *being*, it's never been a thing to *have*. The universe has an infinite flow of everything ... and we mean *everything*. When you transform yourself, and come into alignment with your life, you'll see there's enough of everything for everyone. When you trust that the universe is always supporting you and will bring you everything you ask for (if you stay in alignment with it!), the flow of abundance will manifest in your life very quickly.

On a more practical level, if we want to change the world, having wealth and abundance in our lives does make our mission easier. Some people say, *'You don't need money to make an impact.'* That's true in many cases, yet it sure helps. Having money enables you to mobilize resources, people and ideas more quickly, and have a bigger impact. It also allows you to share the wealth with others.

We hope that for you, gathering wealth means more than buying Christian Louboutin shoes or a snazzy red sports car (both of which we want you to desire and enjoy too)! When you're clear what the wealth is for, it will manifest so quickly and so abundantly that you might surprise yourself.

How to Transform Your Money Story

What happens to your energy when you think about money? Do you clam up, get scared or paralysed? Does that feel like the right vibration to be sending out to the universe? We need to transform our feelings about money so we feel expanded emotions about it consistently. Follow the Five Steps of EAM to release the resistance in your energy. With Step 5, allow yourself to align to receiving more abundance on all levels.

Your Money Mindset

One of the easiest ways to begin raising your abundance set point is to work on your money mindset. We wish there was space in this book to share all the many common money mindset beliefs and patterns that stand in your way! Such as, '*I find it hard to save money*', '*I spend money as soon as I get it*', and '*I believe I don't have enough money.*' What do you find yourself thinking, saying or mulling over in your head time and time again?

Take a look at what money really means to you. What do you believe having money will bring you? What emotion do you believe you'll feel when you have it? Use the sway to ask questions around money and then use the Five Steps of EAM to let go of the beliefs and meanings you've attached to it and to transform any resistant energy. By doing this you can align to the positive meanings and connect to allowing a flow of money into your life.

Maybe you've had experiences in your past where you lost money, were in debt, or made money and had to sacrifice something to get it. You'll have a story about money, good or bad. The question is, does your money story support or hinder you? If you know you have a story going on, then it's time for you to do the work. By changing your money story, you also change your reality around wealth and abundance.

Element 8 Exercise –
Be an Energetic Millionaire

When working with the universe, no one pops out of the sky and leaves a map on your desk to tell you how to get there. Your guidance comes as little signals, messages, thoughts, words and actions. When inspired ideas come to you, write them down. Then take action! Take at least one step toward making it happen.

It really IS time to change. If you want a new money story to come true then start doing, thinking and saying things differently. Just for a minute close your eyes, relax and get the feeling of abundance in your body. Affirm, 'I AM a millionaire' until you get a big sway forward (if you sway backward then release resistance first until you sway forward). If you knew that next year, or in six months, you'd be a millionaire no matter what you did, write down the answers to the following:

What's the new powerful story that you want to create to tell yourself and everyone else? Think about what you do for a living in your new story. How much money do you earn? How long has it taken you to create it? How much free time have you got? How easy is it to work? How much support do you have? Use the sway to help you construct this story to get clear on the details. Use Step 5 to align to the answers you have to these three questions:

- What would you THINK differently?
- What would you DO differently?
- What would you SAY differently?

Element 9 –
Finding Your Passion and Purpose

Here you'll discover how to use your energy to follow your heart, live your purpose and create or define your mission in life. We're still working to expand those outer layers of our aura and connect to our purpose in the wider world, whether you're here to do bookkeeping or save animals, to collect recycling or feed starving children. Each and every single job we have is important. This is about expressing yourself, connecting to your passion and living your life on purpose.

Most people believe their purpose is about what they *do* in the world, that it's something external. Many people spend more time at work than they do at home, in a job they hate, so they can make ends meet, dreaming of a day when they can truly live their passion. Or they go on an endless search for a job title or promotion, push and sacrifice themselves to get there, only to realize they're still unhappy. Your purpose is something inside of you that, once expressed, you get to do in the outside world.

Let's first explore what energy, thoughts and beliefs you hold about being able to find or live your passion in life. What do you believe is in the way of you living your passion? Do you believe you have a purpose? Use the bubble method and the Five Steps of EAM to explore and align to being able to find and live your passion and purpose.

In Elements 9 and 10, your mission is to bring it all to life. You want to create a life, job or business that excites the pants off you *and* is of service to others. You do that by being super clear who you are, what you want to do and who you want to work with. When you're clear and make these decisions then life can send you the people and opportunities to support you.

If you wait for outside circumstances to change you'll never be 'ready'. Your journey so far has been about aligning to this. You've done so much of the inner work already. Now it's time for you to take action and step outside your 'outer limit'. Allow your purpose and passion to lead you in the right direction in your life.

Find Your Passion, Purpose and People

Being on **purpose** is what's authentic to you. Your purpose is about who you are rather than your job title. For example, your purpose may be to teach, lead or inspire. If we create a living based on anything else, it creates a level of resistance. Our mission is to transform that and align ourselves in every way possible. This applies to more than your work; it's every area of your life, and if you're spending over 30% of your life working in some way, surely you want to be happy and in flow. Imagine how the world will be when everyone is living their purpose, happily doing what they love, serving the people they care about. What a different place the world will be.

Your **passion** is important for the same reason, it's about the message you hold. It will be something you're passionate about, meaning you can talk about it all day. You could stand on a soapbox and talk about it to everyone. For us, it's about change and transformation – that is our passion. Everything we do is about that. Passion is a receptive emotion, so when you're living, working and sharing your passion, it's a wonderful way to keep yourself in alignment for 30% of your life.

One of the underlying needs everyone is searching for is connection with other **people**. This could be our children, parents, friends, family, partner or clients. When you look at any impactful experience in life, it's usually to do with our connection with others. We're made to connect, to play our part within a group of people. Right now, the world needs more people who are connected to their purpose, who understand their passion and the people they want to support. Are you ready for that to be you?

To find your purpose, ask yourself what values in life are important to you. What do you believe is needed in the world? How can you turn that into work or a business? The first and most important step is for you to discover your purpose. To be clear: your purpose is about *why* you do something, rather than what you do for a living. Your work is more like the application of your purpose; it's the *how*.

There will be something (maybe more than one thing) that you're passionate about. It's something that you feel compelled to do. Usually, it's something you want to change or that you can see a new way of doing. Often this comes from your own journey: it's your story. Your passion is about discovering what really lights you up. It can also be a way that you express yourself; for example, art, music, painting or speaking.

Finally, every person needs to know what values they live by. Your personal core values will map across into your work or business and become the ethics by which you live. What makes your work unique is you! Be clear on your personal values, aim to summarize them down to 10 core values that apply to every area of your life.

Find Your People

Part of living your passion and purpose includes being part of a community of people who need you most. Who is ready to hear your message? To evolve and grow, it's important to be in a community, or work with a team of people, on a similar mission, whether you join one that already exists or create your own. What's wonderful about the universe is that your team is already gathered somewhere. You just have to find them or bring them to you, energetically.

This now leads us to the community of people you want to make a difference to. You have a natural gift or talent that others need. As a leader, or someone who wants to make a difference, it's up to you to see the potential in them and keep that vision of what's possible in their future alive (even when they have given up). It's then that you have something to give.

Use the sway to define the traits you want to see in people around you and in your work community. Align yourself to attracting the traits you need. Create a list of people to connect with. Who can enable you to achieve your vision? Who do you know that can support you in getting to where you want to be? What communities can you be a part of who will understand you?

Element 9 Exercise – Discover Your Purpose

You may want to use this space to discover your purpose in life. Use the following questions to explore this topic:

- What do you find yourself doing all the time in every situation?
- When you look back, what have all of your job roles included? Is there a theme?
- When you were at school, what did you find yourself doing the most? (It doesn't have to have been in the classroom.)
- What do you get so engrossed in that you forget to eat?

- What do you spend your time fantasizing about?
- From these questions does there emerge a key theme? Are there two or three words or qualities that draw them all together?
- Using the sway ask, 'Is this my purpose?'

Now use the sway to help you get clear on this and release any resistance to discovering your purpose. Remember the most important thing in every situation is *who* you are, rather than *what* you do.

Element 10 – Making Your Impact

Now we're at the edge of our energetic experience. How will you really show up in the world, take action and put your life's work into practice? Now that you've done all the work in the previous elements, you're ready to create the massive impact, financial success and recognition you want and deserve. This is the greatest expansion of ourselves; we're beyond the edge of our energy field and now using our aligned and expanded self to make our difference in the world.

Whether you're working for yourself or working for someone else, the important part is that *you* are making your difference. You can live your passion and make an impact inside an organization just as much as you can by building your own business. You've been through this entire journey. It probably feels like a million years ago since we first began doing the work on getting you in alignment, working on your resistances, aligning your energy structures, and looking at the thoughts and beliefs that have been standing in your way.

We hope that by now you're feeling like an entirely different person and your life should be looking very different, too. Of course, this has just been a tiny introduction to what's possible with EAM.

What is making an impact really all about? For us, making your impact is important whether you influence 10 people, 100 people or a million people. It's about the difference that only *you* can make. We hope the work life you're now designing is coming from a place of alignment, that it's coming from vision, your heart, understanding yourself, your mission, your story and all of the experiences that have brought you to this point in your life.

If you're yet to start doing work that is meaningful to you, now is the time. If you're already doing that, then hopefully this might give you some more ideas that you can tweak or share, or new perspectives. As we spend 30% of our life at work, let's be sure you enjoy that time, and stay in alignment as much as possible every day.

Why do we need to make an impact? If you aren't doing what you love for work, you're spending 30% of your life out of flow. Most people in the world get up every day and go to work. They hate their job. They hate their business. They get stressed out. They feel overwhelmed and tired. They spend time and energy dreaming of winning the lottery, so that they can be free. They believe that money = freedom. We know that freedom is a choice. What if you took the leap and did that anyway? We have one life, so f***ing live it. If you are, or have been, spending years of your life doing work that you hate, please stop. The world needs you to listen to that calling in your heart.

How do we get in alignment with the work that we want to do? This is about looking at the practical action steps that we need to take. Remember your life needs to be in alignment. Everything we've done so far in the Energy Evolution journey has been about bringing your alignment level up. Now, more than ever, you need to ensure that your energy, vision, thoughts, words, emotions and actions are all in alignment to raise your frequency. Unless you're putting yourself out there, sharing your big vision, doing work that's meaningful to you, how can the universe respond to that and the other areas of your life? Why would it, if you're living out of alignment with yourself?

Clearing Hurdles and Creating a Business in Flow

Look at the perceived hurdles and obstacles that you think may get in your way. Maybe that's technology, family, or waiting for money, skills, knowledge or expertise around work or business. Perhaps you know your passion, maybe you feel you need more training or qualifications to really go out there and support people. Whatever your hurdles, identify them now. Once you let go of the belief, that's when the magic can truly start to happen.

What are your perceived hurdles? Sometimes it might be a very practical answer, not an energetic answer. For example, if you need to build a Facebook fan page, you need to find out how to do that. Other people might be able to connect you with somebody or make a recommendation. Sometimes the solution is outside of us and all you need is someone to point you in the right direction.

Whether you're running a business, finding clients, aiming to work for a charitable cause, or needing to convince the boss that you're the one to run a project, you'll have to find a way to educate people and deliver an idea that is fun, engaging and educational. You'll need to get people to buy into what it is you want to share. You want them to understand your story, to love what you do and know your message, which means they go out and spread the word on your behalf. It's a win when people know what you do because you never know when they are going to start sharing your message with somebody else.

Use the sway to help you identify three key messages that you wish everyone would know. If you could stand on your soapbox and shout at everyone, what would you say? Use the Five Steps of EAM and align yourself to sharing this message and embodying it so it emanates from you.

Practise this. If you have an important presentation to do, do yourself the honour of practising what you're about to share. Make sure you're in alignment with your words. Use EAM to work through any resistance, so that when you share, it comes from a place of alignment. You want to make sure your message is congruent, that it feels right for you, and it's what you believe. Work on releasing any resistance about anything you're sharing with others, particularly if you're inviting people to buy from you or take some action. Resistance travels, even through the internet. Our voice, our energy and our passion is all communicated just as much through the internet as when you're meeting somebody face to face. If you're out of alignment, in the wrong energy when you record something, feeling resistant, or feeling scared or overwhelmed, that all transfers as well. You want to make sure that you're as receptive and as prepared as possible.

So, if you have a big presentation, event or talk where you need to speak, make sure you're aligned to your words. Use the Five Steps of EAM to release any resistance and align to them hearing the true meaning of your message, so that they take the action you need them to.

This last element was really looking at the outside world, at what makes you sing. How are you creating your wealth and making an impact in the world? Everything is energy and it all begins with the emotions, thoughts and beliefs we hold about every area of our lives. Now you've expanded yourself and your energy out to be in alignment on every level of your aura, your life will be feeling *far* more in flow.

Element 10 Exercise – What Are You Here For?

It's time to be truthful with yourself and to align to what you are here to do. If you need to, go back and listen to your visualization to connect to your impact in the world. Use the sway to ask questions and get ideas about what you are meant to do for your work. Do you know what it is yet? Has it been shown to you? Do you need to wait, or take some action to find it? Unless you're doing it already, align yourself to knowing what you're here for and start taking action toward it. Write down your vision, what you feel or know. Use your sway to help you clarify if those statements or intentions are true and aligned for you. Of course, release any resistance and align to everything you're asking for.

Chapter 9

CHANGING THE WORLD
WITH EAM

What a journey we've been on. While we hope that it's been an epic adventure for you too, this is really just the beginning. In this last chapter, let's explore what's possible when we come together. What we can do when the world is aligned and in flow? What could you do better with a community to support and people who understand you?

You Are Limitless

Our basic human nature is growth and expansion; the universe was created that way. We are born to want more and be successful. We find ourselves looking at the future sometimes with hope or hopelessness, sometimes with fear or joy. We all have a dream, a vision, something we're aiming for, whether that dream means having one more day off a week or living on a beach in Barbados. It's a projection of ourselves and our lives in the future.

Life is constant journey of expansion. If we're expanding, by definition there's a limit to where we are right now. Imagine it's like an edge or an outer or upper limit. Energetically, we're talking about the *edge* of our aura and what's contained within it. To allow more into our lives, we have to move beyond our

247

current limitations. These limitations show up as self-sabotage and are designed to keep us safe. They kick in when we reach the outer edge of our current self-imposed bubble – and you're about to break through!

We'll always have an upper limit. No matter how 'successful' you are or what you're aiming for, there'll always be a limit on your current potential because it's the boundary line of our current capacity. Self-imposed limits created by your current mindset, thoughts, beliefs and experiences. Every time you break through your 'glass ceiling' onto the next level, there'll be another to greet you. The good news is that your next glass ceiling will be way beyond your current experience, so you have plenty of room to expand.

This is why EAM is focused on releasing any and all resistance: so you can continually expand. The better your life gets, the more your capacity to receive improves.

Our limitations come in many ways, usually by doing what's out of alignment. When we have these hidden barriers in place, we'll find a way to ruin situations around us even when life is going great. These are all just resistances or reversals created by unresolved issues in our aura. These could be in the form of beliefs, stuck emotions, memories we hold or stories we keep on telling. There's no end to what form the limitation may take.

Now, with EAM, you can recognize when these limitations are showing up, transform them and stop them sabotaging your efforts to change your life. First, let go of the pattern of allowing these self-imposed limits to kick in, so that you can prevent yourself from creating more of these situations. Then, when they occur, celebrate! It's a chance to step beyond the limit – you can use EAM to break the 'hidden barrier' and step into your next level of alignment.

Ascension – Awaken to Your Heart

As we move beyond the fear, you'll begin to see, feel and experience a life beyond the normal day-to-day. The journey we've talked about throughout this book is more than just working through the Energy Evolution. We all arrive on earth on a journey, from birth to our transition at death. This is a journey of evolution and growth, for us to experience the situations that are presented to us to learn from, if we choose. Many people refer to this as your spiritual journey, soul's journey, life path or your ascension.

Ascension means, 'the act of raising to a higher level or a movement upward', and is a perfect description of what's happening to you. Using EAM can create changes in our body and biofield as it evolves through a process that allows you to vibrate at a higher frequency. As we work through the Energy Evolution and other journeys with EAM, this can start to really develop your awareness, which can trigger a further awakening for many.

In the process of your frequency upgrading, you move into a higher consciousness, which emanates more light or source energy outward. Remember at the beginning we talked about all energy being light waves? This is what's meant when people say, 'shine your light'. It's a personal journey, an awareness of your soul, your mission and, most importantly, your connection to source. Then we change how we interact with the world around us, which can have a profound effect on your daily life.

As your vibration starts to change, your sense of knowing, seeing, feeling, hearing and understanding adapts – you feel in tune. You connect at a deeper level with the wonder of the world around you, and you'll see how we are all connected in this universe.

Ascension is a different experience for everyone. In the world of light and energy, time doesn't exist as we all are vibrating at different frequencies. We're here to return to our own truth, our authentic self. We learn to integrate our light and dark, and learn we're all the same. We're peeling back the layers and identifying all the baggage we learned growing up and what we brought into this lifetime. The purpose of ascension is to 'remember' who we really are. We're allowing space for our higher selves to integrate with our physical body. This brings a true connection to source and we see all aspects of reality.

That is a whole other book in itself. We're mentioning it here simply to open the door to what is possible. As our physical body becomes free of restrictions, we absorb and hold more light. This happens by cellular restructure and changes in our DNA. We activate the four Rs: rewiring, refining, rewriting and re-establishing. This starts with *rewiring* our cellular structure. The journey is about *refining* our DNA; we get to *rewrite* the script by working with our biofields and aligning both the spiritual and physical; then we start to *re-establish* the codes – the memories in our blueprint – for a deeper understanding. In the physical, we can start to notice signs of our frequency or vibration changing. We may think they're illnesses or conditions; however, frequently they're physiological signs of changes. Here are some signs you may notice when you start your bio-dynamic integration:

- Your 'clair' senses become much more tuned in. For example, **clairvoyance** ('clear seeing'), **clairaudience** ('clear hearing'), **claircognizance** ('clear knowing') and **clairsentience** ('clear feeling').
- Knowing there is something different about you.
- Frequency changes in the ears.
- Feeling more sensitive and emotional.

- More headaches, especially around the third eye, back of head and crown chakra.
- Sleep disruption and vivid dreams.
- Questions around your mission or purpose in life
- Unexplained chest pains, aches in the body or teeth.
- Our environment around us can change as our frequency expands.
- Life drama or situations occur which can be a big karmic release.
- Materialism might become less important to you.
- You're no longer dealing with the 'ego'.
- Recognizing synchronicity and signs around you.
- Eyesight changes as it adapts.

We're altering the physical body to bring more light in and greater vibrations of energy. This means you become a beacon of light, love and magnetism. Simply by your presence, you'll create change on an energetic level. This is such a deep subject, for now we wanted you to have a glimpse of the basics, in case they start to occur. You can use EAM to work on all of these symptoms and know they are signs of change. If you're concerned about anything, always consult a professional. Remember, each stage of ascension is about a new experience for you and the involvement that your body, soul and spirit will go through. This is your journey into a whole new world.

Align to the Right Resources

To create the success you want, it's vital to find the right resources and support. If you feel you need more support, time or money as well as doing the energy work, there are some practical actions you can take.

Let's find some time in your life. Look at what you spend time doing and ask yourself, is it important to me? Do I love it? Is it taking me toward my vision? If the answer to any of these things is no, then let it go. It starts from the moment you wake up. Do you lie in bed in the morning scrolling through Facebook on your phone, or do you write in your journal and make a plan for your day? Do you watch TV, play video games, listen to the news or read magazines? What could you listen to or choose to read instead? If you commute, do you listen to inspiring books or training on your journey or do you people watch or play on your phone?

What do you do while cooking dinner, gardening or putting washing on? Maybe you could get up an hour earlier or go to bed an hour later? What if you asked a friend to look after the kids for an extra afternoon? What if you asked everyone to chip in more around the house? What roles are you playing that are sucking up more of your time and energy? Could you hire a cleaner for two hours a week to bring you more time? What could you achieve with it? We all have the same 24 hours in the day. It's what you choose to do with them that counts.

Do you know anyone who created their success alone? Even the greatest people in history had support and the right resources to build their achievements. We all have a wealth of responsibilities in our lives, and you can only be in one place at a time. If you have children and you're at work, do you leave them on their own? No, of course not. You get support with childcare or school. At work, when you're stuck do you ask help from someone who has never done it? Or someone who loves it, and has a passion and understanding for it? Think about a child at school. Do you expect them to know everything the first day, or do you provide them with support, and people to guide them and enable them to learn?

The same goes for changing your life. We *all* need guidance along the way. It's up to you to put the right resources and support strategies in place. How will you prioritize yourself to get the energy, time and money to implement these changes in your life?

Find the right guide, support and love around you.

In general, you will find that other people are more than willing to support us. It's usually us who struggle to ask for it. If you had more time to get yourself in flow, how would that ultimately benefit you and your family? Maybe you need external support and guidance. What skills, knowledge or expertise do you need around you? What mental and emotional support do you have? We know sometimes the people around us think this stuff is crazy! On the journey, how can you get the right support from the right people? Ask yourself, *what* resources do I need and *how* am I going get them to change my life, once and for all?

Be With the Right People

Research into bioenergetics (the study of energy relationships and transformations of living organisms) show that energy sources such as algae can take and absorb energy from one another and their environment. We do the same thing.

Have you ever noticed that when you change your environment to something more peaceful you feel better? Or when you're with certain people you feel uneasy or uncomfortable. That's because we can absorb energy from other people, too. In fact, we absorb energy all the time. So, who you spend time with is very important because you literally 'soak up' their frequency.

It's vital to your success to have the right people around who do get it! Do you have some people in your life who'd laugh at everything in this book? Maybe share it with others first. If you're easily knocked, swayed or influenced by others, hang out with people who think and feel the same as you or bring you higher.

If it's right for you, and people around you will get it, share EAM with them. Share it with your children, family and friends. The more people around you who are doing it, that you can talk to or bounce ideas off, the better it will be for you.

While EAM *is* a self-help tool that you can absolutely use on your own, it's also nice to be part of a community of people who understand it, have done it and can support you in changing your life. You're never alone, and the greatest successes come from allowing others to support you. If you want to be with us and other light-hearted people who are putting EAM into practice, join us here: www.energyalignmentmethod.com/join-the-community.

It's said that we're the average of the five people we most associate with. We know energetically this is true. Studies have shown that our energy will synchronize to the highest frequency in the room. So, if you're spending a lot of time with people who drag you down, it's easy to jump on their bandwagon, or to spend all your time bringing the energy up. Even when we *know* we're surrounded by people who bring us down, we tend to stay there because it's 'safe' and what we know.

On the flip side, when you spend time with people who inspire, lift you up and show you what is possible, they empower your progress to change your life. Your aligned action is to surround yourself with people who have the same or a higher vibrational energy and viewpoint of life. You'll soon see how quickly your frequency is lifted up.

Take some aligned action. How can you be part of a group or community of people who have the same or higher vibration than you? Maybe join a local meet-up group, support network or healing circle. Whether it's online or in person, ideally get yourself in a room where you're in the energy field of others who are in alignment. Come to a live EAM event – it's an indescribable experience!

Trying to Change Others

If we want to change the world, we'd best have our own foundations in place. This means being in alignment first. By bringing all elements of yourself and your life into alignment, your needs get met internally. You no longer need anyone or anything outside of you. They are there in your life through choice, instead of necessity.

This is exactly what the Energy Evolution is all about, and this was a simple introduction to a much wider piece of work. We hope the work you've done in this book has brought you a new level of alignment. As you start looking to help other people around you, first put on your own oxygen mask. If you want to give to others when you're out of flow, you'll have nothing to give. Once you've brought yourself into alignment, you'll have the energy and capacity to support others because energy will flow through you instead of from you. Allow yourself to recognize and meet your own needs first.

Let's face it, life would be easier if everyone agreed with us! Yet the world would be a boring place if they were. It's this interplay of energy between us all that creates the differences in our lives. To change our lives, we have to change the way we interact with others, too. We're going to have to learn to live with 'other' people who are yet to meet the new paradigm! Instead of expecting them to change to make us happy, we'll do the work to make ourselves happy no matter what they say or do.

Dealing with people who are still living in the old paradigm can be difficult. They may use blame, shame, guilt, push, pull and manipulation to get your attention. You may still find yourself getting dragged back into those ways of communicating, too. It can be hard, believe us, we know. Instead of judging, simply recognize it as another opportunity to do EAM. You can change the frequency, and live in the new paradigm in all your relationships (with or without the people in your life right now).

When you're able to recognize your own interactions, and choose to respond in a different way, the 'stuff' that other people do will no longer influence or impact your state. Guess what, as soon as your vibration changes, you'll see the shifts inside them, too. That is when the true magic with EAM begins as you see the impact of your frequency shifts changing others.

As you go on the journey to changing your life, other people will have lots of opinions about what you ought to do. The truth is, it will be down to you. Your choice is to always come from the place of alignment.

Let's talk about the way we see other people. If we see something in someone else that is pushing our buttons, it's more about us than it is about them. Many of the feelings, thoughts and emotions you hold are about what happened in the past, rather than what's happening in your present. Those situations may be to do with that person directly or someone they remind you of. Either way, we have to own our 'stuff' and do the work on it. So, before we can have clear and aligned communication, connection or relationship with them we have to clear up our energy about them first. Otherwise, it's all clouded with resistant thoughts and emotions!

This has an awesome two-way benefit. Working on yourself releases it from your energy field, so there is nothing to refire later. As you clear your emotional and mental filters, you'll receive their message more clearly.

Remember in our Step 5 aligned energy, our aura expands; it is strong and complete. This means that nothing and no one can mess with you. In Step 5, you're in the state of love, which is the highest vibration and the foundation of new paradigm living.

Make a new choice today. It all begins with working on your own vibrational frequency. You may notice that people are different with you. Or you'll hear them say, 'You've changed'. It's almost as if they find it hard to understand what's different, or they may want to drag you back into their story. When you stay in alignment, they'll try even harder to pull you back to the metaphorical dark side! Stay strong and use the light energetic force!

In all our years working with thousands of people, we know one of the biggest wastes of your time and energy is the crazy notion that you can change someone else! If we push someone to change, we're creating more resistance in the relationship. Energetically, you're pushing their energy field, which makes them feel small. We all want to be as expanded as possible, so they'll automatically push back. Every single time. So, what do you do?

Imagine if we put the energy we give to others into changing ourselves. If you *really* want to see change that's exactly what you need to do. Our lives would change more quickly than we can possibly imagine. Use that energy to change the situation instead. You have the power to change the dynamic in the relationship and let that stress, push, pull or tension go. If there are people in your life who you wish would change, follow what you've learned in this book. Show yourself how powerful you are. You'll find magic in using EAM to change your relationship with others. As your frequency shifts, they'll change too.

Working With a Coach or Mentor

When thinking about the right support, you may also want to consider getting yourself a guide. Are we saying for you to come and work with us? Yes and no. Everyone needs to find the right guide for them. There are some really important aspects to consider and it's about much more than the letters they have after their name.

Let's take this back to energy. Our physical body is one big sensory unit. It's designed to pick up, receive and understand information from our environment, internally and externally. We're also able to pick up on the frequency of others – this energy can influence us and we can influence it. It's happening with every person and every interaction. This knowledge is crucial to understand from both sides when you're looking for a coach, guide or mentor, or if you're already someone, or would like to be someone, in those roles. Here's why.

We often think of 'coaching' to be the ability to ask those deep questions, watch for facial movements, notice tonality of the voice, subtle body movements, gestures and ticks. It's well-documented that people who are in a deep or meaningful connected conversation will start to mirror one another, we do this all the time in everyday communication. Yet there's something else happening – we become energetically linked to the people we connect with. Research shows that when our heart is coherent and we're communicating with others there is increased physiological linkage; we become more sensitive to others, enabling a greater connection to occur.

Also, the power of working with someone face-to-face (in person or online) activates the limbic system, which reduces the effects of stress and trauma in the body from current or past experiences. Again, these are powerful effects, which happen by being in the presence of someone, especially if they are leading you in a coaching role. Therefore, the energy of the coach, mentor or therapist you choose to work with is of great importance to you. Studies have now shown that their vibration has an impact on the level of changes that can be made on physiological and psychological states of their clients, just by their presence. This can work for and against you. What's actually happening is a silent energetic communication between each person's heart energy; when in rapport and in each other's presence, there's a synchronization of heart wave flows. Hearts will synchronize to the highest frequency in the room.

So, what does this mean for you when choosing a guide? In terms of expansion, you want your guide to have a higher frequency than you, meaning they've done the energy work on themselves. It's never about them having more money or external success than you. You need to know their frequency is higher, allowing you to expand your energy to reach that level and beyond.

If you are a coach, therapist or mentor already, we invite you to ask yourself the question: have you truly done the level of work on yourself and your own energy? Have you invested in yourself enough to shift the imprints you're carrying in order to be an even brighter energetic presence to transform the lives of your clients? We believe it's our duty to do so.

Think about it for a second: would you go to a fitness instructor who was overweight or go to a dentist with bad teeth? Would you trust a schoolteacher who couldn't spell? You get the idea. Choosing your coach, mentor or guide is exactly the same. You need to know that the person you're trusting to guide you on your journey has the skill, knowledge and experience, and the energetic capacity, to expand you. This is why all of our mentors have to go on their own journey of transformation prior to the in-depth EAM training on how to use it in practice with others.

Now of course if you'd like to work with one of our amazing EAM mentors, you would have someone to guide you who has been on this journey and walks their talk. We have an ever-expanding team with a wide range of expertise in every field. They're standing by, ready to guide you as you put this into practice. Visit www.energyalignmentmethod.com/coaching/ for more information.

Become a Mentor

Have you been feeling that nudge inside you? Maybe reading this book and seeing transformations, you've felt the difference EAM can make in your life and the lives of others. Whether you're already a therapist, coach, mentor or guide, or even if you've never done anything like this before, if there is a tug inside of you, we invite you to listen. It's known as 'the call'.

Becoming an EAM mentor is no small journey. It's a self-exploration and expansion voyage like no other, even before we train you to put this powerful tool into practice with others. It's about being able to walk your talk, having done the work and uplevelled your own vibration in order to support others.

Our mentors who are already therapists, coaches or mentors in other modalities have said that EAM is like nothing else they've trained in for creating the shifts in their clients. It complements and accelerates their transformations to the next level. Even for those who've never done anything like this before, from the first level of their training they and their clients have been amazed at the shifts that just one session can bring because they have chosen to let go. That said, if you're already in a practice, as tempting as it may be to start sharing all you've learned with clients, please know that this is entry-level EAM in the book – there is a lot more to learn if you want to mentor support or guide others. In addition, you'd need to be qualified and accredited to do so. So, if this rings your heart, find out more.

Going on a journey alone to change the world can feel tough at times. We can spend a long time alone, trying to make a difference – with a team we can do so much more. More importantly, being an EAM mentor is also about the sense of belonging, the friendships, the lifelong support and teamwork and living in the new paradigm. It's empowering to have people who have faith in you especially at those times when you've no faith in yourself.

Think about the growth of anything. The luminaries you recognize now in any industry were often the pioneers who were part of the journey from the beginning. Right now, EAM is pretty new; if you're feeling the calling, it's probably for a reason. It could be part of your path. It's no coincidence that you're reading this book.

You Can Change the World

For a second let's take it back to the science of life. Have you ever seen those awesome pictures that pull you into a never-ending pattern as you look closer? This type of picture is called a fractal. It's a repeating pattern that never ends: whichever level you look at, it's the same. Almost everything in nature can be discussed as a fractal. Science has shown that our natural world is built on these incredible fractal patterns.

Our universe is made up of millions of galaxies. Inside each galaxy are millions of solar systems, which contain millions of planets, which contain millions of moons, clouds, rocks, rivers and possibly life. On our own earth, this fractal pattern has been seen in rivers and tributaries, coastlines and mountain ranges, as well as the construct of clouds, seashells and hurricanes. It's the same in our physical body. We see ourselves as one human being working independently. Yet we only need to use a microscope to see that we're in fact one organism made up of – some crazy number – like 37 trillion cells. Each of those cells is made up of a crazy number of atoms and proteins and electrons. Whichever level you look at, we're creating this fractal-based community of living energy. Health and sickness on one level is reflected across all levels of the fractal community.

Let's take that understanding and expand it out from us as individuals. We live in households, communities, towns, cities and countries; we all populate this one giant organism, planet earth. Together, we're one community. What affects one part of our community affects it all. When we all come back to it, everything is energy – remember we all come from one source connected by this one field of electromagnetic energy. The health and well-being of the planet is, in fact, directly connected and affected by the spiritual, mental, emotional and physical health and wellbeing of us as individuals and vice versa. It is our collective energetic health vibration and evolution as a human race.

Become a Silent Rebel

As you go about your daily activity, having done this work and used EAM on yourself and raised your vibration, you are thinking, living, feeling and being in the new paradigm.

You know the world is filled with abundance, see the good in everything and everyone as amazing things happen. Even when the bad experiences happen, you bounce back in a way like never before. We want you to know YOU ARE CHANGING the planet, simply by your presence. You are a *light walker*!

You can change the world, be a light walker.

Now, the people on this planet are calling out for change, we know we want something – different, fairer, kinder, more loving – maybe we're yet to be clear what it is. So, people fight, scream, protest and riot to get attention. There is another way for us to do this. Be a silent rebel.

Our silent rebel philosophy is grounded in being the change itself. Instead of creating change in the old paradigm, we have to first become it, then create the new life or world from that place. Our bigger mission behind EAM and the work we're doing is to be part of this global transformation. To empower people to wake up, to provide the tools, ideas, community and vision to create change in a whole new way.

A silent rebel is far from a pushover – it's someone who knows the new world they want and how to create it. Instead of pointing the finger, placing blame, putting more resistance, anger and attention on the situation as it is (which we know will only create more of it), they focus their energy, attention, time, money and conversation on what is becoming. We KNOW that the old ways never work.

It's about shifting into the new paradigm. Get clear on what you want. What does that look like? How would you love the education system, food, money, employment, travel, politics, healthcare, travel, family life to be? This begins with the journey you've taken and beyond this book with EAM.

Simply for now, be the light wherever you are. As excited as you'll be to share EAM with everyone, they may be ready now or later. Do EAM wherever you are for the people around you, on the train, in the supermarket, in a queue, in traffic, in an online community. Release the resistance wherever you are and fill it with love. You have nothing to say – simply be it, create these pockets of change wherever you go.

Using EAM is creating change on many levels of your own physical, mental, emotional and spiritual health. It will ripple out to change the lives of your family, friends and community. When there are enough of us doing EAM, we'll have an impact on the population of our planet. In other words, *you* can change the world.

Remember, the bigger EAM mission is to empower a global wave of people to step into their power so we can change the world from the old paradigm to the new. This is about bringing in a new way of living: one that is empowering, healthy and sustainable for every being on this planet, plants, animals and humans alike. After everything that life has provided for us, we believe we can play our part in maintaining this beautiful ecosystem. We hope that this book is the beginning, and now you know changing your life with EAM *is* changing the world, too.

For the Next Generation

Imagine a life growing up where you'd known about your inner power and how to align with it from an early age. How different would your life have been if you'd understood the power you have to let go of the pain, hurt, anger, trauma and sadness you experienced from the time you were a child?

Imagine what it'd be like to have a world where all parents knew how to communicate with their children from love, who created safe, respectful boundaries, and who empowered their children to recognize their abilities. How different would the world be right now? How different would your life be?

We have the opportunity right now to create this world for the thousands of children who are born every day. We're on a mission to share EAM as far as possible, to impact the world now and for future generations to come. We know in our hearts that one day soon EAM will be in every school and we'll see people swaying everywhere! Hold that intention and help make it happen.

Create the New Paradigm

You can also change the old paradigm to the new with your work, whatever you *do*. Because it's about who you are *being* when you *do* it. Have you ever sat on the train and had a happy attendant singing away or sending you good wishes on your commute? Or seen a wonderful smile from the cashier as you paid for your shopping? Think about the teacher who inspires a child to recognize they're capable of much more. 'Changing the world' means making one small change. Be in alignment wherever you are. Talk about the good in your life. Inspire people with hope and possibility. Show people it's possible to change their lives and shift what they think and feel.

If you are called to do something that makes a difference, please follow your heart. We both ignored our inner calling for many years. We both knew we wanted to do energy work, but we had no idea what it was. Our lives felt like a push, and never really changed until we stepped fully into what we were meant to do. And wow, what a journey it's been. You're here to share your story and journey with those who need to hear it. You have insight like no one else on this planet because no one else has lived your life. It's for you to share that message. If you feel a call inside, we'd love to help you share your gifts. We hope this book has resonated with you and there is much more we can do.

You have everything in your hands to change your life. With EAM, that transformation will be accelerated. You have limitless resources available to you. Now you know how to tap into this wealth of abundance whenever you choose, promise you'll use it to change your life.

Nothing in this world is broken; it is *all* in the process of change. Right now, we're seeing the chaos as we move to the new paradigm. To change the world, hang out with people of the same vibration, come together to shift the frequency. By doing the work that you've done, and we hope you'll continue to do, with EAM you're contributing to the change in mass consciousness.

Silently rebel and create the change wherever you go. You are here right now on this planet for a reason. Choose to be the solution. We chose this time to experience this. Together we can create this global transformation. Are you ready?

ACKNOWLEDGMENTS

We'd like to start by thanking you for connecting with this book. Allowing your heart to open and trust us to explore this with a little more depth.

To the thousands of participants who took part in our formative research studies into the use of EAM. You helped us to understand the questions that needed to be answered. You bared your souls and changed your lives. Thank you for making EAM what it is today.

To the friends, family and loved ones who have been there through it all. The ups, the downs, the tears, the heartache, the late nights, the early mornings and things you all gave up or contributed to helping to get EAM out there in your own ways.

To our incredible (and growing) team of clients and EAM mentors: we wish we could name you all one by one. You have truly inspired us to keep on going. Watching the shifts and changes in you and seeing the people you have become has been such a privilege. Thank you for hearing your calling and stepping up to take EAM out into the world.

To Jo Lal, Becky Miles and the team at Welbeck Balance for bringing us into your community, your mission and the changes you are helping to create in the world. So excited to see how this all unfolds.

To the thousands of experts, researchers, scientists, philosophers and luminaries who have dedicated their lives to changing the way we live. To those who have trodden the path and shared their wisdom so that we could speed up our own journey, we thank you for making this knowledge so freely available so that we all have the potential to change our lives.

To all the soul family of EAM past, present and future. The team who we work with who hold the vision and light. We are all one and equal in this new way forward

Yvette: And, of course, my wonderful little man, Kye. I have already thanked you. Without you being gifted into our lives, who knows where we would be. This book is for you and all the other children growing up in the new paradigm.

Lisa Hammond, my 'wife', my best friend and partner in creation. EAM would never be what it is without you. It is an honour to share this crazy journey with you. And maybe in this lifetime we'll finally change the world.

Lisa: To my parents, Alan and Dorothy, who I can feel close to me, thank you for the love, lessons and inspiration. To be able to come back and give this life of service. To Yvette, it took us a while to find each other again in this lifetime but it is always divinely timed. So many treasured moments and so much more to come. To Mayan, who I dedicate this legacy we leave behind, to show you what is possible. To all my dear and close family and friends for your love, support and all the lessons. xx

For those friends and family, colleagues, associates or people from our past. Even though your name may be missing, please know that your time, love, energy and connection played a huge part this journey.

RESOURCES AND REFERENCES

Throughout the book we've explored so many people, cited studies and other places you can explore in more depth. Below is a short list from each chapter.

Chapter 1

Bruce, A (2006), *Beyond the Bleep* (Disinformation Company)

Kotler, S and Whelan, J (2017), *Stealing Fire: How Silicon Valley, the Navy SEALs, and Maverick Scientists Are Revolutionizing the Way We Live and Work* (Dey Street Books)

Lipton, B (2015), T*he Biology of Belief* (Hay House)

Chapter 2

Lipton, B (2002), *Nature, Nurture & The Power of Love* (DVD, Jenny Myers Productions)

Chapter 3

Armour, J A and Ardell, J L (eds) (1994), *Neurocardiology* (Oxford University Press)

Bower, G H, 'Mood-congruity of social judgements' in Forgas, J P (ed) (1991), *Emotion and Social Judgments* (Pergamon Press)

Cameron, O G (2002), *Visceral Sensory Neuroscience: Interception* (Oxford University Press)

Childre, D and Rozman, D (2003), *Transforming Anger: The Heart Math Solution for Letting Go of Rage, Frustration, and Irritation* (New Harbinger)

Childre, D and Rozman, D (2005), *Transforming Stress: The Heart Math Solution to Relieving Worry, Fatigue, and Tension* (New Harbinger)

Damasio, A (2004), *Looking for Spinoza: Joy, Sorrow, and the Feeling Brain* (Vintage)

LeDoux, J (1989), 'Cognitive-emotional interactions in the brain', *Cognition and Emotion*, 3(4), pp. 267-89

LeDoux, J (1999), *The Emotional Brain: The Mysterious Underpinnings of Emotional Life* (W&N)

McCraty, R (2003), 'The Energetic Heart Bioelectromagnetic Interactions Within and Between People', *The Neuropsychotherapist*, 6(1), pp. 22-43

McCraty, R and Zayas, M A (2014), 'Cardiac coherence, selfregulation, autonomic stability, and psychosocial well-being', *Frontiers in Psychology*, 5(1090)

Pribram, K H and McGuinness, D (1975), 'Arousal, activation, and effort in the control of attention', *Psychological Review*, 82(2), pp. 116-49

Randoll, U (1992), 'The role of complex biophysical-chemical therapies for cancer', *Bioelectrochemistry and Bioenergetics*, 27(3), pp. 341-46

Rein, G and McCraty, R (1993), 'Modulation of DNA by coherent heart frequencies', *Proceedings of the Third Annual Conference of the International Society for the Study of Subtle Energy and Energy Medicine*, pp. 58-62

Rein, G and McCraty, R (1994), 'Structural changes in water and DNA associated with new physiologically measurable states', *Journal of Scientific Exploration*, 8(3), pp. 438-39

Chapter 4

Chevalier, G *et al* (2012), 'Earthing: Health Implications of Reconnecting the Human Body to the Earth's Surface Electrons', *Journal of Environmental and Public Health*

Damasio, A R (2006), *Descartes' Error: Emotion, Reason and the Human Brain* (Vintage)

Hicks, E and Hicks, J (2020), *The Astonishing Power of Emotions* (Hay House)

Labonte, M L and Prevost, N (1998), *Wings of Light, The Art of Angelic Healing* (Blue Pearl Press)

Lindgren, C E, Litt, D and Baltz, J (1997), *Aura Awareness* (Blue Dolphin Publishing)

Pennington, A (2016), *The Orgasm Prescription for Women* (Make Your Mark Global)

Reichstien, G (1999), *Wood Becomes Water: Chinese Medicine in Everyday Life* (Kodansha America)

Scaer, R (2012), *8 Keys to Brain-Body Balance* (WW Norton & Co)

Stefanov, M *et al* (2013), 'The Primo Vascular System as a New Anatomical Systems', *Journal of Acupuncture and Meridian Studies*, 6(6), pp. 331-38

Watts, E (2019), *Cosmic Ordering Made Easier* (Wilson King Publishing)

Chapter 5

Alia-Klein, N, Goldstein, R Z *et al* (2007), 'What is in a Word? No versus Yes Differentially Engage the Lateral Orbitofrontal Cortex', *Emotion*, 7(3), pp. 649-59

Garrie, T (2013), *The Act of Attraction in Business* (Panoma Press)

Hawkins, D R (2004), *Power Vs Force* (Hay House)

McCraty, R (2003), 'Heart-brain neurodynamics: The making of emotions', *The Neuropsychotherapist*, 6(1), pp. 68-89

McCraty, R *et al* (1998), 'The impact of a new emotional selfmanagement program on stress, emotions, heart rate variability, DHEA and cortisol', *Integrative Physiological and Behavioural Science*, 33(2), pp. 151-70

Stanley, R (2009), 'Types of prayer, heart rate variability and innate healing', *Journal of Religion and Science*, 44(4), pp. 825-46

Chapter 8
Emoto, M (2005), *The Hidden Messages in Water* (Pocket Books)
Fisslinger, J R (2018), *The 6 Root-Cause(s) Of All Symptoms: Fear No More. Know WHY you've symptoms with Lifestyle Prescriptions* (CreateSpace)
Hay, L (1984), *You Can Heal Your Life* (Hay House)
Pert, C (1999), *Molecules of Emotion: Why You Feel the Way You Feel* (Simon & Schuster)
Rose, E (2013), Metaphysical Anatomy (CreateSpace)
Shaperio, D (1990), *The Bodymind Workbook* (Thorsons)

Chapter 9
Hendricks, G (2010), *The Big Leap* (HarperOne)
Lipton, S and Bhaerman, S (2011), *Spontaneous Evolution* (Hay House)
McCraty, R, Atkinson, M, Tomasino, D and Tiller, W A (1998), 'The electricity of touch: Detection and measurement of cardiac energy exchange between people', in *Brain and Values* (Psychology Press)

TAKE YOUR NEXT STEPS WITH EAM

Now you know the Five Steps of EAM and how to make them work. You can begin to understand more on how to apply these to your life. There is so much more to EAM than we can share with you in this book. If you're really ready to change your life and start putting all of this into practice, visit our website: www.energyalignmentmethod.com

You can find out more or book a call to discover more about our transformational workshops, retreats and online programmes. Here are just a few:

- Energy Experience – Fear To Love
- Energy Express – Introductory live EAM workshop
- Energy Exploration – How to Change Your Life
- Energy Expansion – Raise Your Vibration 5 Day Intensive
- Energy Education – Advanced EAM Training
- EAM Mentor Accreditation – Qualify to Teach and Share EAM with Others

You'll find out how to explore those key subjects in more depth in the Energy Evolution. Come find our library of ideas and insights on:

- Expand Your Love – Reclaim Your Power, Transform Relationships
- Creating More Money, Wealth and Abundance
- Exploring Sex, Love and Power of Your Hara

- Create Your Attractive Vision
- 121 Empowerment Sessions with an EAM Mentor

Just follow the links here to explore and find out more www.energyalignmentmethod.com

We are so excited to see you there, let's take this next step to change your life and the wider world together.

ABOUT WELBECK BALANCE

Welbeck Balance publishes books dedicated to changing lives. Our mission is to deliver life enhancing books to help improve your wellbeing so that you can live your life with greater clarity and meaning, wherever you are on life's journey. Our Trigger books are specifically devoted to opening up conversations about mental health and wellbeing.

Welbeck Balance and Trigger are part of the Welbeck Publishing Group – a globally recognised independent publisher based in London. Welbeck are renowned for our innovative ideas, production values and developing long-lasting content. Our books have been translated into over 30 languages in more than 60 countries around the world.

Find out more at:
www.welbeckpublishing.com
Twitter.com/welbeckpublish
Instagram.com/welbeckpublish
Facebook.com/welbeckuk

Find out more about Trigger at:
www.triggerhub.org
Twitter.com/Triggercalm
Facebook.com/Triggercalm
Instagram.com/Triggercalm

WELBECK
BALANCE